LECTIONARY FOR MASS

THE ROMAN MISSAL
RENEWED BY DECREE OF THE
MOST HOLY SECOND ECUMENICAL COUNCIL OF THE VATICAN,
PROMULGATED BY AUTHORITY OF POPE PAUL VI
AND REVISED AT THE DIRECTION OF POPE JOHN PAUL II

LECTIONARY FOR MASS

FOR USE IN THE DIOCESES
OF THE UNITED STATES OF AMERICA

SECOND TYPICAL EDITION

Supplement

COMMITTEE ON DIVINE WORSHIP
UNITED STATES CONFERENCE OF CATHOLIC BISHOPS

2017

A Liturgical Press Book

LITURGICAL PRESS COLLEGEVILLE, MINNESOTA

Concordat cum originali:

✠ Wilton D. Gregory
Chairman, USCCB Committee on Divine Worship
after review by Rev. Michael J. Flynn
Executive Director, USCCB Secretariat of Divine Worship

Published by the authority of the Committee on Divine Worship,
United States Conference of Catholic Bishops

Design by Frank Kacmarcik, Obl.S.B.

Published by Liturgical Press, Collegeville, Minnesota. Printed in the United States of America.

ISBN 978-0-8146-4513-0 (Classic Edition)
ISBN 978-0-8146-4537-6 (Chapel Edition)

CONTENTS

PREFACE

The Fathers of the Second Vatican Council called for an expansion of the Scripture readings available for the Holy Mass, so that the faithful who participate in the Eucharist might be nourished by a greater number and variety of biblical texts. In response, the Holy See issued the *Ordo Lectionum Missæ* in 1969 and promulgated a revised and expanded second edition in 1981. The four volumes of the current *Lectionary for Mass for Use in the Dioceses of the United States of America*, published between 1998 and 2002, are based on that Latin second typical edition.

In 2001 and again in 2015, the Congregation for Divine Worship and the Discipline of the Sacraments issued updates to the *Ordo Lectionum Missæ* to account for recent changes to the Liturgy of the Roman Rite: an expanded Vigil Mass for Pentecost, celebrations of saints added to the General Roman Calendar, and the addition of new Votive Masses. Revisions to the Proper Calendar for the Dioceses of the United States of America have also taken place, necessitating further changes to the Lectionary.

Therefore, the United States Conference of Catholic Bishops' Committee on Divine Worship approved the publication of this *Lectionary for Mass Supplement* in June 2015. Until the publication of a future edition of the *Lectionary for Mass*, this Supplement will provide a convenient source for the texts of readings for the occasions listed above.

"Let the word of Christ dwell in you richly" (Col 3:16). May the *Lectionary for Mass Supplement* be a valuable resource for parishes and liturgical ministers, so that the words of Saint Paul, first addressed to the Church in Colossae, may also encourage the Church in the United States to savor God's word more deeply and so to grow in holiness.

✠ Arthur J. Serratelli
Chairman, Committee on Divine Worship
United States Conference of Catholic Bishops
(2013–2016)

PROPER OF TIME

SACRED PASCHAL TRIDUUM AND EASTER TIME

62 PENTECOST SUNDAY

AT THE VIGIL MASS

(In churches where the Vigil Mass is celebrated in the simple form, see vol. I, no. 62.)

In churches where the Vigil Mass is celebrated in an extended form, the readings with their proper Psalms are proclaimed in the following order:

FIRST READING

Genesis 11:1-9 It was called Babel because there the LORD confused the speech of all the world.

A reading from the Book of Genesis

The whole world spoke the same language, using the same words.
While the people were migrating in the east,
they came upon a valley in the land of Shinar and settled there.
They said to one another,
"Come, let us mold bricks and harden them with fire."
They used bricks for stone, and bitumen for mortar.
Then they said, "Come, let us build ourselves a city
and a tower with its top in the sky,
and so make a name for ourselves;
otherwise we shall be scattered all over the earth."

The LORD came down to see the city and the tower
that the people had built.
Then the LORD said: "If now, while they are one people,
all speaking the same language,
they have started to do this,
nothing will later stop them from doing whatever they presume to do.

Let us then go down there and confuse their language,
so that one will not understand what another says."
Thus the LORD scattered them from there all over the earth,
and they stopped building the city.
That is why it was called Babel,
because there the LORD confused the speech of all the world.
It was from that place that he scattered them all over the earth.

The word of the Lord.

RESPONSORIAL PSALM

Psalm 33:10-11, 12-13, 14-15

℟. (12) **Blessed the people the Lord has chosen to be his own.**

The Lord brings to nought the plans of nations;
he foils the designs of peoples.
But the plan of the Lord stands forever;
the design of his heart, through all generations.

℟. **Blessed the people the Lord has chosen to be his own.**

Blessed the nation whose God is the Lord,
the people he has chosen for his own inheritance.
From heaven the Lord looks down;
he sees all mankind.

℟. **Blessed the people the Lord has chosen to be his own.**

From his fixed throne he beholds
all who dwell on the earth,
He who fashioned the heart of each,
he who knows all their works.

℟. **Blessed the people the Lord has chosen to be his own.**

SECOND READING

Exodus 19:3-8a, 16-20b The LORD came down upon Mount Sinai before all the people.

A reading from the Book of Exodus

Moses went up the mountain to God.
Then the LORD called to him and said,
"Thus shall you say to the house of Jacob;
tell the Israelites:
You have seen for yourselves how I treated the Egyptians
and how I bore you up on eagle wings
and brought you here to myself.
Therefore, if you hearken to my voice and keep my covenant,
you shall be my special possession,
dearer to me than all other people,
though all the earth is mine.
You shall be to me a kingdom of priests, a holy nation.
That is what you must tell the Israelites."
So Moses went and summoned the elders of the people.
When he set before them
all that the LORD had ordered him to tell them,
the people all answered together,
"Everything the LORD has said, we will do."

On the morning of the third day
there were peals of thunder and lightning,
and a heavy cloud over the mountain,
and a very loud trumpet blast,
so that all the people in the camp trembled.
But Moses led the people out of the camp to meet God,
and they stationed themselves at the foot of the mountain.
Mount Sinai was all wrapped in smoke,
for the LORD came down upon it in fire.

**The smoke rose from it as though from a furnace,
and the whole mountain trembled violently.
The trumpet blast grew louder and louder, while Moses
was speaking,
and God answering him with thunder.**

**When the LORD came down to the top of Mount Sinai,
he summoned Moses to the top of the mountain.**

The word of the Lord.

RESPONSORIAL PSALM

Daniel 3:52, 53, 54, 55, 56

℟. (52b) **Glory and praise for ever!**

"Blessed are you, O Lord, the God of our fathers,
praiseworthy and exalted above all forever;
And blessed is your holy and glorious name,
praiseworthy and exalted above all for all ages."

℟. **Glory and praise for ever!**

"Blessed are you in the temple of your holy glory,
praiseworthy and glorious above all forever."

℟. **Glory and praise for ever!**

"Blessed are you on the throne of your Kingdom,
praiseworthy and exalted above all forever."

℟. **Glory and praise for ever!**

"Blessed are you who look into the depths
from your throne upon the cherubim,
praiseworthy and exalted above all forever."

℟. **Glory and praise for ever!**

"Blessed are you in the firmament of heaven,
praiseworthy and glorious forever."

℟. **Glory and praise for ever!**

OR:

Psalm 19:8, 9, 10, 11

℟. (John 6:68c) **Lord, you have the words of everlasting life.**

The law of the LORD is perfect,
refreshing the soul;
The decree of the LORD is trustworthy,
giving wisdom to the simple.

℟. **Lord, you have the words of everlasting life.**

The precepts of the LORD are right,
rejoicing the heart;
The command of the LORD is clear,
enlightening the eye.

℟. **Lord, you have the words of everlasting life.**

The fear of the LORD is pure,
enduring forever;
The ordinances of the LORD are true,
all of them just.

℟. **Lord, you have the words of everlasting life.**

They are more precious than gold,
than a heap of purest gold;
Sweeter also than syrup
or honey from the comb.

℟. **Lord, you have the words of everlasting life.**

THIRD READING

Ezekiel 37:1-14 Dry bones of Israel, I will bring spirit into you, that you may come to life.

A reading from the Book of the Prophet Ezekiel

The hand of the LORD came upon me,
and he led me out in the spirit of the LORD
and set me in the center of the plain,
which was now filled with bones.
He made me walk among the bones in every direction
so that I saw how many they were on the surface of the plain.
How dry they were!
He asked me:
Son of man, can these bones come to life?
I answered, "Lord GOD, you alone know that."
Then he said to me:
Prophesy over these bones, and say to them:
Dry bones, hear the word of the LORD!
Thus says the Lord GOD to these bones:
See! I will bring spirit into you, that you may come to life.
I will put sinews upon you, make flesh grow over you,
cover you with skin, and put spirit in you
so that you may come to life and know that I am the LORD.
I, Ezekiel, prophesied as I had been told,
and even as I was prophesying I heard a noise;
it was a rattling as the bones came together, bone joining bone.
I saw the sinews and the flesh come upon them,
and the skin cover them, but there was no spirit in them.
Then the LORD said to me:
Prophesy to the spirit, prophesy, son of man,
and say to the spirit: Thus says the Lord GOD:
From the four winds come, O spirit,
and breathe into these slain that they may come to life.

I prophesied as he told me, and the spirit came into them;
they came alive and stood upright, a vast army.
Then he said to me:
Son of man, these bones are the whole house of Israel.
They have been saying,
"Our bones are dried up,
our hope is lost, and we are cut off."
Therefore, prophesy and say to them: Thus says the Lord GOD:
O my people, I will open your graves
and have you rise from them,
and bring you back to the land of Israel.
Then you shall know that I am the LORD,
when I open your graves and have you rise from them,
O my people!
I will put my spirit in you that you may live,
and I will settle you upon your land;
thus you shall know that I am the LORD.
I have promised, and I will do it, says the LORD.

The word of the Lord.

RESPONSORIAL PSALM

Psalm 107:2-3, 4-5, 6-7, 8-9

℟. (1) **Give thanks to the Lord; his love is everlasting.**
or:
℟. **Alleluia.**

Let the redeemed of the LORD say,
those whom he has redeemed from the hand of the foe
And gathered from the lands,
from the east and the west, from the north and the south.

℟. **Give thanks to the Lord; his love is everlasting.**
or:
℟. **Alleluia.**

They went astray in the desert wilderness;
the way to an inhabited city they did not find.
Hungry and thirsty,
their life was wasting away within them.

℟. **Give thanks to the Lord; his love is everlasting.**
or:
℟. **Alleluia.**

They cried to the LORD in their distress;
from their straits he rescued them.
And he led them by a dircct way
to reach an inhabited city.

℟. **Give thanks to the Lord; his love is everlasting.**
or:
℟. **Alleluia.**

Let them give thanks to the LORD for his mercy
and his wondrous deeds to the children of men,
Because he satisfied the longing soul
and filled the hungry soul with good things.

℟. **Give thanks to the Lord; his love is everlasting.**
or:
℟. **Alleluia.**

FOURTH READING

Joel 3:1-5 I will pour out my spirit upon the servants and handmaids.

A reading from the Book of the Prophet Joel

Thus says the LORD:
I will pour out my spirit upon all flesh.
Your sons and daughters shall prophesy,
your old men shall dream dreams,
your young men shall see visions;
even upon the servants and the handmaids,
in those days, I will pour out my spirit.
And I will work wonders in the heavens and on the earth,
blood, fire, and columns of smoke;
the sun will be turned to darkness,
and the moon to blood,
at the coming of the day of the LORD,
the great and terrible day.
Then everyone shall be rescued
who calls on the name of the LORD;
for on Mount Zion there shall be a remnant,
as the LORD has said,
and in Jerusalem survivors
whom the LORD shall call.

The word of the Lord.

RESPONSORIAL PSALM

Psalm 104:1-2, 24 and 35, 27-28, 29-30

℟. (cf. 30) **Lord, send out your Spirit, and renew the face of the earth.**

or:

℟. **Alleluia.**

Bless the Lord, O my soul!
O Lord, my God, you are great indeed!
You are clothed with majesty and glory,
robed in light as with a cloak.

℟. **Lord, send out your Spirit, and renew the face of the earth.**

or:

℟. **Alleluia.**

How manifold are your works, O Lord!
In wisdom you have wrought them all—
the earth is full of your creatures;
bless the Lord, O my soul! Alleluia.

℟. **Lord, send out your Spirit, and renew the face of the earth.**

or:

℟. **Alleluia.**

Creatures all look to you
to give them food in due time.
When you give it to them, they gather it;
when you open your hand, they are filled with good things.

℟. **Lord, send out your Spirit, and renew the face of the earth.**

or:

℟. **Alleluia.**

If you take away their breath, they perish
and return to their dust.
When you send forth your spirit, they are created,
and you renew the face of the earth.

℟. **Lord, send out your Spirit, and renew the face of the earth.**
or:
℟. **Alleluia.**

EPISTLE

Romans 8:22-27 The Spirit intercedes with inexpressible groanings.

A reading from the Letter of Saint Paul to the Romans

Brothers and sisters:
We know that all creation is groaning in labor pains even until now;
and not only that, but we ourselves,
who have the firstfruits of the Spirit,
we also groan within ourselves
as we wait for adoption, the redemption of our bodies.
For in hope we were saved.
Now hope that sees is not hope.
For who hopes for what one sees?
But if we hope for what we do not see, we wait with endurance.

In the same way, the Spirit too comes to the aid of our weakness;
for we do not know how to pray as we ought,
but the Spirit himself intercedes with inexpressible groanings.
And the one who searches hearts
knows what is the intention of the Spirit,
because he intercedes for the holy ones
according to God's will.

The word of the Lord.

ALLELUIA

℟. **Alleluia, alleluia.**

**Come, Holy Spirit, fill the hearts of your faithful
and kindle in them the fire of your love.**

℟. **Alleluia, alleluia.**

GOSPEL

John 7:37-39 Rivers of living water will flow.

✠ **A reading from the holy Gospel according to John**

**On the last and greatest day of the feast,
Jesus stood up and exclaimed,
"Let anyone who thirsts come to me and drink.
As Scripture says:
Rivers of living water will flow from within him who believes in me."**

**He said this in reference to the Spirit
that those who came to believe in him were to receive.
There was, of course, no Spirit yet,
because Jesus had not yet been glorified.**

The Gospel of the Lord.

PROPER OF SAINTS

JANUARY 3

510/1 THE MOST HOLY NAME OF JESUS

FIRST READING

Philippians 2:1-11 God bestowed on him the name that is above every name.

A reading from the Letter of Saint Paul to the Philippians

Brothers and sisters:
If there is any encouragement in Christ,
any solace in love,
any participation in the Spirit,
any compassion and mercy,
complete my joy by being of the same mind,
with the same love, united in heart,
thinking one thing.
Do nothing out of selfishness or out of vainglory;
rather, humbly regard others as more important than yourselves,
each looking out not for his own interests, but also everyone for those of others.
Have among yourselves the same attitude
that is also yours in Christ Jesus,
Who, though he was in the form of God,
did not regard equality with God something to be grasped.
Rather, he emptied himself,
taking the form of a slave,
coming in human likeness;
and found human in appearance,
he humbled himself,
becoming obedient to death,
even death on a cross.

Because of this, God greatly exalted him
and bestowed on him the name
that is above every name,
that at the name of Jesus
every knee should bend,
of those in heaven and on earth and under the earth,
and every tongue confess that
Jesus Christ is Lord,
to the glory of God the Father.

The word of the Lord.

RESPONSORIAL PSALM

Psalm 8:4-5, 6-7, 8-9

℟. (2ab) **O Lord, our God, how wonderful your name in all the earth!**

When I behold your heavens, the work of your fingers,
the moon and stars which you set in place—
What is man that you should be mindful of him,
or the son of man that you should care for him?

℟. **O Lord, our God, how wonderful your name in all the earth!**

You have made him little less than the angels,
and crowned him with glory and honor.
You have given him rule over the works of your hands,
putting all things under his feet.

℟. **O Lord, our God, how wonderful your name in all the earth!**

All sheep and oxen,
yes, and the beasts of the field,
The birds of the air, the fishes of the sea,
and whatever swims the paths of the seas.

℟. **O Lord, our God, how wonderful your name in all the earth!**

ALLELUIA

Matthew 1:21

℟. **Alleluia, alleluia.**

You are to name him Jesus,
because he will save his people from their sins.

℟. **Alleluia, alleluia.**

GOSPEL

Luke 2:21-24 The child was named Jesus.

✠ **A reading from the holy Gospel according to Luke**

When eight days were completed for his circumcision,
the child was named Jesus, the name given him by the angel
before he was conceived in the womb.

When the days were completed for their purification
according to the law of Moses,
they took him up to Jerusalem
to present him to the Lord,
just as it is written in the law of the Lord,
Every male that opens the womb shall be consecrated to
***the Lord*,**
and to offer the sacrifice of
***a pair of turtledoves or two young pigeons*,**
in accordance with the dictate in the law of the Lord.

The Gospel of the Lord.

JANUARY 6

[In the Dioceses of the United States]

510C SAINT ANDRÉ BESSETTE, RELIGIOUS

From the Common of Holy Men and Women: For Religious (vol. II, III, or IV, nos. 737–742).

JANUARY 22*

(*January 23, when January 22 falls on a Sunday)

[In the Dioceses of the United States]

516A DAY OF PRAYER FOR THE LEGAL PROTECTION OF UNBORN CHILDREN

From the Masses for Various Needs and Occasions, III. In Various Public Circumstances: 26A. For Giving Thanks to God for the Gift of Human Life (Supplement, nos. 947A–947E, pg. 117), or II. For Public Needs: 14. For Peace and Justice (vol. IV, nos. 887–891).

JANUARY 23

[In the Dioceses of the United States]

517 SAINT VINCENT, DEACON AND MARTYR

In the United States, this Optional Memorial is transferred to this date from January 22.

From the Common of Martyrs (vol. II, III, or IV, nos. 713–718), or:

FIRST READING

2 Corinthians 4:7-15 Always carrying about in the body the dying of Jesus.

A reading from the second Letter of Saint Paul to the Corinthians

Brothers and sisters:
We hold this treasure in earthen vessels,
that the surpassing power may be of God and not from us.
We are afflicted in every way, but not constrained;
perplexed, but not driven to despair;
persecuted, but not abandoned;
struck down, but not destroyed;
always carrying about in the body the dying of Jesus,
so that the life of Jesus may also be manifested in our body.
For we who live are constantly being given up to death
for the sake of Jesus,
so that the life of Jesus may be manifested in our mortal flesh.

So death is at work in us, but life in you.

Since, then, we have the same spirit of faith,
according to what is written, *I believed, therefore I spoke*,
we too believe and therefore speak,
knowing that the one who raised the Lord Jesus
will raise us also with Jesus
and place us with you in his presence.
Everything indeed is for you,
so that the grace bestowed in abundance on more and more people
may cause the thanksgiving to overflow for the glory of God.

The word of the Lord.

RESPONSORIAL PSALM

Psalm 34:2-3, 4-5, 6-7, 8-9

℟. (5) **The Lord delivered me from all my fears.**

I will bless the LORD at all times;
his praise shall be ever in my mouth.
Let my soul glory in the LORD;
the lowly will hear me and be glad.

℟. **The Lord delivered me from all my fears.**

Glorify the LORD with me,
let us together extol his name.
I sought the LORD, and he answered me
and delivered me from all my fears.

℟. **The Lord delivered me from all my fears.**

Look to him that you may be radiant with joy,
and your faces may not blush with shame.
When the afflicted man called out, the LORD heard,
and from all his distress he saved him.

℟. **The Lord delivered me from all my fears.**

The angel of the LORD encamps
around those who fear him, and delivers them.
Taste and see how good the LORD is;
blessed the man who takes refuge in him.

℟. **The Lord delivered me from all my fears.**

ALLELUIA

Matthew 5:10

℟. **Alleluia, alleluia.**

**Blessed are they who are persecuted for the sake of righteousness,
for theirs is the Kingdom of heaven.**

℟. **Alleluia, alleluia.**

GOSPEL

Matthew 10:17-22 You will be led before governors and kings for my sake as a witness before them and the pagans.

✠ **A reading from the holy Gospel according to Matthew**

**Jesus said to his Apostles:
"Beware of men, for they will hand you over to courts
and scourge you in their synagogues,
and you will be led before governors and kings for my sake
as a witness before them and the pagans.
When they hand you over,
do not worry about how you are to speak
or what you are to say.
You will be given at that moment what you are to say.
For it will not be you who speak
but the Spirit of your Father speaking through you.
Brother will hand over brother to death,
and the father his child;
children will rise up against parents and have them put to death.
You will be hated by all because of my name,
but whoever endures to the end will be saved."**

The Gospel of the Lord.

JANUARY 23

[In the Dioceses of the United States]

517A SAINT MARIANNE COPE, VIRGIN

From the Common of Virgins (vol. II, III, or IV, nos. 731–736), or the Common of Holy Men and Women: For Those Who Work for the Underprivileged (vol. II, III, or IV, nos. 737–742).

FEBRUARY 8

529A SAINT JOSEPHINE BAKHITA, VIRGIN

From the Common of Virgins (vol. II, III, or IV, nos. 731–736), or:

FIRST READING

1 Corinthians 7:25-35 A virgin is anxious about the things of the Lord.

A reading from the first Letter of Saint Paul to the Corinthians

Brothers and sisters:
In regard to virgins, I have no commandment from the Lord,
but I give my opinion as one who by the Lord's mercy is trustworthy.
So this is what I think best because of the present distress:
that it is a good thing for a person to remain as he is.
Are you bound to a wife? Do not seek a separation.
Are you free of a wife? Then do not look for a wife.
If you marry, however, you do not sin,
nor does an unmarried woman sin if she marries;
but such people will experience affliction in their earthly life,
and I would like to spare you that.

I tell you, brothers, the time is running out.
From now on, let those having wives act as not having them,
those weeping as not weeping,
those rejoicing as not rejoicing,
those buying as not owning,
those using the world as not using it fully.
For the world in its present form is passing away.

I should like you to be free of anxieties.
An unmarried man is anxious about the things of the Lord,
how he may please the Lord.

But a married man is anxious about the things of the world,
how he may please his wife, and he is divided.
An unmarried woman or a virgin is anxious about the things of the Lord,
so that she may be holy in both body and spirit.
A married woman, on the other hand,
is anxious about the things of the world,
how she may please her husband.
I am telling you this for your own benefit,
not to impose a restraint upon you,
but for the sake of propriety
and adherence to the Lord without distraction.

The word of the Lord.

RESPONSORIAL PSALM

Psalm 45:11-12, 14-15, 16-17

℟. (11) **Listen to me, daughter; see and bend your ear.**
or:
℟. **The bridegroom is here; let us go out to meet Christ the Lord.**

Hear, O daughter, and see; turn your ear,
forget your people and your father's house.
So shall the king desire your beauty;
for he is your lord, and you must worship him.

℟. **Listen to me, daughter; see and bend your ear.**
or:
℟. **The bridegroom is here; let us go out to meet Christ the Lord.**

All glorious is the king's daughter as she enters;
her raiment is threaded with spun gold.
In embroidered apparel she is borne in to the king;
behind her the virgins of her train are brought to you.

℟. **Listen to me, daughter; see and bend your ear.**
or:
℟. **The bridegroom is here; let us go out to meet Christ the Lord.**

They are borne in with gladness and joy;
they enter the palace of the king.
The place of your fathers your sons shall have;
you shall make them princes through all the land.

℟. **Listen to me, daughter; see and bend your ear.**
or:
℟. **The bridegroom is here; let us go out to meet Christ the Lord.**

ALLELUIA

℟. **Alleluia, alleluia.**

This is the wise virgin, whom the Lord found waiting;
at his coming, she went in with him to the wedding feast.

℟. **Alleluia, alleluia.**

GOSPEL

Matthew 25:1-13 Behold, the bridegroom! Come out to meet him!

✠ **A reading from the holy Gospel according to Matthew**

Jesus told his disciples this parable:
"The Kingdom of heaven will be like ten virgins
who took their lamps and went out to meet the bridegroom.
Five of them were foolish and five were wise.
The foolish ones, when taking their lamps,
brought no oil with them,
but the wise brought flasks of oil with their lamps.
Since the bridegroom was long delayed,
they all became drowsy and fell asleep.
At midnight, there was a cry,
'Behold, the bridegroom! Come out to meet him!'
Then all those virgins got up and trimmed their lamps.
The foolish ones said to the wise,
'Give us some of your oil,
for our lamps are going out.'
But the wise ones replied,
'No, for there may not be enough for us and you.
Go instead to the merchants and buy some for yourselves.'
While they went off to buy it,
the bridegroom came
and those who were ready went into the wedding feast with him.
Then the door was locked.
Afterwards the other virgins came and said,
'Lord, Lord, open the door for us!'
But he said in reply,
'Amen, I say to you, I do not know you.'
Therefore, stay awake,
for you know neither the day nor the hour."

The Gospel of the Lord.

MAY 10

[In the Dioceses of the United States]

561A SAINT DAMIEN DE VEUSTER, PRIEST

From the Common of Pastors (vol. II, III, or IV, nos. 719–724), or the Common of Holy Men and Women (vol. II, III, or IV, nos. 737–742).

MAY 13

563A OUR LADY OF FATIMA

From the Common of the Blessed Virgin Mary (vol. II, III, or IV, nos. 707–712), or:

FIRST READING

Isaiah 61:9-11 I rejoice heartily in the LORD.

A reading from the Book of the Prophet

Thus says the LORD:
Their descendants shall be renowned among the nations,
and their offspring among the peoples;
All who see them shall acknowledge them
as a race the LORD has blessed.

I rejoice heartily in the LORD,
in my God is the joy of my soul;
For he has clothed me with a robe of salvation,
and wrapped me in a mantle of justice,
Like a bridegroom adorned with a diadem,
like a bride bedecked with her jewels.
As the earth brings forth its plants,
and a garden makes its growth spring up,
So will the Lord GOD make justice and praise
spring up before all the nations.

The word of the Lord.

RESPONSORIAL PSALM

Psalm 45:11-12, 14-15, 16-17

℟. (11) **Listen to me, daughter; see and bend your ear.**

Hear, O daughter, and see; turn your ear,
forget your people and your father's house.
So shall the king desire your beauty;
for he is your lord, and you must worship him.

℟. **Listen to me, daughter; see and bend your ear.**

All glorious is the king's daughter as she enters;
her raiment is threaded with spun gold.
In embroidered apparel she is borne in to the king;
behind her the virgins of her train are brought to you.

℟. **Listen to me, daughter; see and bend your ear.**

They are borne in with gladness and joy;
they enter the palace of the king.
The place of your fathers your sons shall have;
you shall make them princes through all the land.

℟. **Listen to me, daughter; see and bend your ear.**

ALLELUIA

℟. **Alleluia, alleluia.**

**Blessed are you, holy Virgin Mary, deserving of all praise;
from you rose the sun of justice, Christ our God.**

℟. **Alleluia, alleluia.**

GOSPEL

Luke 11:27-28 Blessed is the womb that carried you.

✠ **A reading from the holy Gospel according to Luke**

**While Jesus was speaking,
a woman from the crowd called out and said to him,
"Blessed is the womb that carried you
and the breasts at which you nursed."
He replied, "Rather, blessed are those
who hear the word of God and observe it."**

The Gospel of the Lord.

MAY 21

566A SAINT CHRISTOPHER MAGALLANES, PRIEST, AND COMPANIONS, MARTYRS

From the Common of Martyrs (vol. II, III, or IV, nos. 713–718), or:

FIRST READING

Revelation 7:9-17 These are the ones who have survived the time of great distress.

A reading from the Book of Revelation

I, John, had a vision of a great multitude,
which no one could count,
from every nation, race, people, and tongue.
They stood before the throne and before the Lamb,
wearing white robes and holding palm branches in their hands.
They cried out in a loud voice:

"Salvation comes from our God, who is seated on the throne,
and from the Lamb."

All the angels stood around the throne
and around the elders and the four living creatures.
They prostrated themselves before the throne,
worshiped God, and exclaimed:

"Amen. Blessing and glory, wisdom and thanksgiving,
honor, power, and might
be to our God forever and ever. Amen."

Then one of the elders spoke up and said to me,
"Who are these wearing white robes, and where did they come from?"
I said to him, "My lord, you are the one who knows."

He said to me,
"These are the ones who have survived the time of great distress;
they have washed their robes
and made them white in the Blood of the Lamb.

"For this reason they stand before God's throne
and worship him day and night in his temple.
The One who sits on the throne will shelter them.
They will not hunger or thirst anymore,
nor will the sun or any heat strike them.
For the Lamb who is in the center of the throne will shepherd them
and lead them to springs of life-giving water,
and God will wipe away every tear from their eyes."

The word of the Lord.

RESPONSORIAL PSALM

Psalm 34:2-3, 4-5, 6-7, 8-9

℟. (5) **The Lord delivered me from all my fears.**

I will bless the LORD at all times;
his praise shall be ever in my mouth.
Let my soul glory in the LORD;
the lowly will hear me and be glad.

℟. **The Lord delivered me from all my fears.**

Glorify the LORD with me,
let us together extol his name.
I sought the LORD, and he answered me
and delivered me from all my fears.

℟. **The Lord delivered me from all my fears.**

Look to him that you may be radiant with joy,
and your faces may not blush with shame.
When the afflicted man called out, the LORD heard,
and from all his distress he saved him.

℟. **The Lord delivered me from all my fears.**

The angel of the LORD encamps
around those who fear him, and delivers them.
Taste and see how good the LORD is;
blessed the man who takes refuge in him.

℟. **The Lord delivered me from all my fears.**

ALLELUIA

Matthew 5:10

℟. **Alleluia, alleluia.**

**Blessed are they who are persecuted for the sake of righteousness,
for theirs is the Kingdom of heaven.**

℟. **Alleluia, alleluia.**

GOSPEL

John 12:24-26 If a grain of wheat falls to the ground and dies, it produces much fruit.

✠ **A reading from the holy Gospel according to John**

Jesus said to his disciples:
"Amen, amen, I say to you,
unless a grain of wheat falls to the ground and dies,
it remains just a grain of wheat;
but if it dies, it produces much fruit.
Whoever loves his life loses it,
and whoever hates his life in this world
will preserve it for eternal life.
Whoever serves me must follow me,
and where I am, there also will my servant be.
The Father will honor whoever serves me."

The Gospel of the Lord.

MAY 22

566B SAINT RITA OF CASCIA, RELIGIOUS

From the Common of Holy Men and Women: For Religious (vol. II, III, or IV, nos. 737–742), or:

FIRST READING

Philippians 4:4-9 Think about whatever is worthy of praise.

A reading from the Letter of Saint Paul to the Philippians

Brothers and sisters:
Rejoice in the Lord always.
I shall say it again: rejoice!
Your kindness should be known to all.
The Lord is near.
Have no anxiety at all, but in everything,
by prayer and petition, with thanksgiving,
make your requests known to God.
Then the peace of God that surpasses all understanding
will guard your hearts and minds in Christ Jesus.

Finally, brothers and sisters,
whatever is true, whatever is honorable,
whatever is just, whatever is pure,
whatever is lovely, whatever is gracious,
if there is any excellence
and if there is anything worthy of praise,
think about these things.
Keep on doing what you have learned and received
and heard and seen in me.
Then the God of peace will be with you.

The word of the Lord.

RESPONSORIAL PSALM

Psalm 1:1-2, 3, 4 and 6

℟. (40:5a) **Blessed are they who hope in the Lord.**
or:
℟. (2a) **Blessed are they who delight in the law of the Lord.**
or:
℟. (92:13-14) **The just will flourish like the palm tree in the garden of the Lord.**

Blessed the man who follows not
the counsel of the wicked
Nor walks in the way of sinners,
nor sits in the company of the insolent,
But delights in the law of the LORD
and meditates on his law day and night.

℟. **Blessed are they who hope in the Lord.**
or:
℟. **Blessed are they who delight in the law of the Lord.**
or:
℟. **The just will flourish like the palm tree in the garden of the Lord.**

He is like a tree
planted near running water,
That yields its fruit in due season,
and whose leaves never fade.
Whatever he does, prospers.

℟. **Blessed are they who hope in the Lord.**
or:
℟. **Blessed are they who delight in the law of the Lord.**
or:
℟. **The just will flourish like the palm tree in the garden of the Lord.**

Not so, the wicked, not so;
they are like chaff which the wind drives away.
For the LORD watches over the way of the just,
but the way of the wicked vanishes.

℟. **Blessed are they who hope in the Lord.**
or:
℟. **Blessed are they who delight in the law of the Lord.**
or:
℟. **The just will flourish like the palm tree in the garden of the Lord.**

ALLELUIA

Matthew 11:28

℟. **Alleluia, alleluia.**

Come to me, all you who labor and are burdened,
and I will give you rest, says the Lord.

℟. **Alleluia, alleluia.**

GOSPEL

Luke 6:27-38 Be merciful, just as your Father is merciful.

✠ **A reading from the holy Gospel according to Luke**

Jesus said to his disciples:
"To you who hear I say,
love your enemies, do good to those who hate you,
bless those who curse you, pray for those who mistreat you.
To the person who strikes you on one cheek,
offer the other one as well,
and from the person who takes your cloak,
do not withhold even your tunic.
Give to everyone who asks of you,
and from the one who takes what is yours do not demand it back.

Do to others as you would have them do to you.
For if you love those who love you,
what credit is that to you?
Even sinners love those who love them.
And if you do good to those who do good to you,
what credit is that to you?
Even sinners do the same.
If you lend money to those from whom you expect repayment,
what credit is that to you?
Even sinners lend to sinners,
and get back the same amount.
But rather, love your enemies and do good to them,
and lend expecting nothing back;
then your reward will be great
and you will be children of the Most High,
for he himself is kind to the ungrateful and the wicked.
Be merciful, just as also your Father is merciful.

"Stop judging and you will not be judged.
Stop condemning and you will not be condemned.
Forgive and you will be forgiven.
Give and gifts will be given to you;
a good measure, packed together, shaken down, and overflowing,
will be poured into your lap.
For the measure with which you measure
will in return be measured out to you."

The Gospel of the Lord.

JULY 1

[In the Dioceses of the United States]

592A SAINT JUNÍPERO SERRA, PRIEST

From the Common of Pastors: For Missionaries (vol. II, III, or IV, nos. 719–724), or the Common of Holy Men and Women: For Religious (vol. II, III, or IV, nos. 737–742).

JULY 5

[In the Dioceses of the United States]

594 SAINT ELIZABETH OF PORTUGAL

In the United States, this Optional Memorial is transferred to this date from July 4.

From the Common of Holy Men and Women: For Those Who Work for the Underprivileged (vol. II, III, or IV, nos. 737–742), or:

FIRST READING

1 John 3:14-18 We ought to lay down our lives for our brothers.

A reading from the first Letter of Saint John

Beloved:
We know that we have passed from death to life
because we love our brothers.
Whoever does not love remains in death.
Everyone who hates his brother is a murderer,
and you know that anyone who is a murderer
does not have eternal life remaining in him.
The way we came to know love
was that he laid down his life for us;
so we ought to lay down our lives for our brothers.
If someone who has worldly means
sees a brother in need and refuses him compassion,
how can the love of God remain in him?
Children, let us love not in word or speech
but in deed and truth.

The word of the Lord.

RESPONSORIAL PSALM

Psalm 112:1-2, 3-4, 5-6, 7-8, 9

℟. (1) **Blessed the man who fears the Lord.**
or:
℟. **Alleluia.**

Blessed the man who fears the Lord,
who greatly delights in his commands.
His posterity shall be mighty upon the earth;
the upright generation shall be blessed.

℟. **Blessed the man who fears the Lord.**
or:
℟. **Alleluia.**

Wealth and riches shall be in his house;
his generosity shall endure forever.
Light shines through the darkness for the upright;
he is gracious and merciful and just.

℟. **Blessed the man who fears the Lord.**
or:
℟. **Alleluia.**

Well for the man who is gracious and lends,
who conducts his affairs with justice;
He shall never be moved;
the just one shall be in everlasting remembrance.

℟. **Blessed the man who fears the Lord.**
or:
℟. **Alleluia.**

An evil report he shall not fear;
his heart is firm, trusting in the LORD.
His heart is steadfast; he shall not fear
till he looks down upon his foes.

℟. **Blessed the man who fears the Lord.**
or:
℟. **Alleluia.**

Lavishly he gives to the poor,
his generosity shall endure forever;
his horn shall be exalted in glory.

℟. **Blessed the man who fears the Lord.**
or:
℟. **Alleluia.**

ALLELUIA

John 13:34

℟. **Alleluia, alleluia.**

I give you a new commandment:
love one another as I have loved you.

℟. **Alleluia, alleluia.**

GOSPEL

Long Form

Matthew 25:31-46 Whatever you did for the least of my brothers, you did for me.

✠ **A reading from the holy Gospel according to Matthew**

Jesus said to his disciples:
"When the Son of Man comes in his glory,
and all the angels with him,
he will sit upon his glorious throne,
and all the nations will be assembled before him.
And he will separate them one from another,
as a shepherd separates the sheep from the goats.
He will place the sheep on his right and the goats on his left.
Then the king will say to those on his right,
'Come, you who are blessed by my Father.
Inherit the kingdom prepared for you from the foundation of the world.
For I was hungry and you gave me food,
I was thirsty and you gave me drink,
a stranger and you welcomed me,
naked and you clothed me,
ill and you cared for me,
in prison and you visited me.'
Then the righteous will answer him and say,
'Lord, when did we see you hungry and feed you,
or thirsty and give you drink?
When did we see you a stranger and welcome you,
or naked and clothe you?
When did we see you ill or in prison, and visit you?'
And the king will say to them in reply,
'Amen, I say to you, whatever you did
for one of the least brothers of mine, you did for me.'

Then he will say to those on his left,
'Depart from me, you accursed,
into the eternal fire prepared for the Devil and his angels.
For I was hungry and you gave me no food,
I was thirsty and you gave me no drink,
a stranger and you gave me no welcome,
naked and you gave me no clothing,
ill and in prison, and you did not care for me.'
Then they will answer and say,
'Lord, when did we see you hungry or thirsty
or a stranger or naked or ill or in prison,
and not minister to your needs?'
He will answer them, 'Amen, I say to you,
what you did not do for one of these least ones,
you did not do for me.'
And these will go off to eternal punishment,
but the righteous to eternal life."

The Gospel of the Lord.

OR:

Short Form

Matthew 25:31-40 Whatever you did for the least of my brothers, you did for me.

✠ **A reading from the holy Gospel according to Matthew**

Jesus said to his disciples:
"When the Son of Man comes in his glory,
and all the angels with him,
he will sit upon his glorious throne,
and all the nations will be assembled before him.
And he will separate them one from another,
as a shepherd separates the sheep from the goats.
He will place the sheep on his right and the goats on his left.
Then the king will say to those on his right,
'Come, you who are blessed by my Father.
Inherit the kingdom prepared for you from the foundation of the world.
For I was hungry and you gave me food,
I was thirsty and you gave me drink,
a stranger and you welcomed me,
naked and you clothed me,
ill and you cared for me,
in prison and you visited me.'
Then the righteous will answer him and say,
'Lord, when did we see you hungry and feed you,
or thirsty and give you drink?
When did we see you a stranger and welcome you,
or naked and clothe you?
When did we see you ill or in prison, and visit you?'
And the king will say to them in reply,
'Amen, I say to you, whatever you did
for one of the least brothers of mine you did for me.'"

The Gospel of the Lord.

JULY 9

596A SAINT AUGUSTINE ZHAO RONG, PRIEST, AND COMPANIONS, MARTYRS

From the Common of Martyrs (vol. II, III, or IV, nos. 713–718), or:

FIRST READING

1 John 5:1-5 The victory that conquers the world is our faith.

A reading from the first Letter of Saint John

Beloved:
Everyone who believes that Jesus is the Christ is begotten by God,
and everyone who loves the Father
loves also the one begotten by him.
In this way we know that we love the children of God
when we love God and obey his commandments.
For the love of God is this,
that we keep his commandments.
And his commandments are not burdensome,
for whoever is begotten by God conquers the world.
And the victory that conquers the world is our faith.
Who indeed is the victor over the world
but the one who believes that Jesus is the Son of God?

The word of the Lord.

RESPONSORIAL PSALM

Psalm 126:1-2ab, 2cd-3, 4-5, 6

℟. (5) **Those who sow in tears shall reap rejoicing.**

When the LORD brought back the captives of Zion,
we were like men dreaming.
Then our mouth was filled with laughter,
and our tongue with rejoicing.

℟. **Those who sow in tears shall reap rejoicing.**

Then they said among the nations,
"The LORD has done great things for them."
The LORD has done great things for us;
we are glad indeed.

℟. **Those who sow in tears shall reap rejoicing.**

Restore our fortunes, O LORD,
like the torrents in the southern desert.
Those who sow in tears
shall reap rejoicing.

℟. **Those who sow in tears shall reap rejoicing.**

Although they go forth weeping,
carrying the seed to be sown,
They shall come back rejoicing,
carrying their sheaves.

℟. **Those who sow in tears shall reap rejoicing.**

ALLELUIA

2 Corinthians 1:3b-4a

℟. **Alleluia, alleluia.**

**Blessed be the Father of compassion and God of all encouragement,
who encourages us in our every affliction.**

℟. **Alleluia, alleluia.**

GOSPEL

John 12:24-26 If a grain of wheat falls to the ground and dies, it produces much fruit.

✠ **A reading from the holy Gospel according to John**

**Jesus said to his disciples:
"Amen, amen, I say to you,
unless a grain of wheat falls to the ground and dies,
it remains just a grain of wheat;
but if it dies, it produces much fruit.
Whoever loves his life loses it,
and whoever hates his life in this world
will preserve it for eternal life.
Whoever serves me must follow me,
and where I am, there also will my servant be.
The Father will honor whoever serves me."**

The Gospel of the Lord.

JULY 14

[In the Dioceses of the United States]

599A SAINT KATERI TEKAKWITHA, VIRGIN
MEMORIAL

From the Common of Virgins (vol. II, III, or IV, nos. 731–736).

JULY 20

601B SAINT APOLLINARIS, BISHOP AND MARTYR

From the Common of Martyrs (vol. II, III, or IV, nos. 713–718), or the Common of Pastors (vol. II, III, or IV, nos. 719–724), or:

FIRST READING

Ezekiel 34:11-16 As a shepherd tends his flock, so will I tend my sheep.

A reading from the Book of the Prophet Ezekiel

Thus says the Lord GOD:
I myself will look after and tend my sheep.
As a shepherd tends his flock
when he finds himself among his scattered sheep,
so will I tend my sheep.
I will rescue them from every place where they were scattered
when it was cloudy and dark.
I will lead them out from among the peoples
and gather them from the foreign lands;
I will bring them back to their own country
and pasture them upon the mountains of Israel
in the land's ravines and all its inhabited places.
In good pastures will I pasture them,
and on the mountain heights of Israel
shall be their grazing ground.
There they shall lie down on good grazing ground,
and in rich pastures shall they be pastured
on the mountains of Israel.
I myself will pasture my sheep;
I myself will give them rest, says the Lord GOD.

The lost I will seek out,
the strayed I will bring back,
the injured I will bind up,
the sick I will heal,
but the sleek and the strong I will destroy,
shepherding them rightly.

The word of the Lord.

RESPONSORIAL PSALM

Psalm 23:1-3a, 4, 5, 6

℟. (1) **The Lord is my shepherd; there is nothing I shall want.**

The LORD is my shepherd; I shall not want.
In verdant pastures he gives me repose;
Beside restful waters he leads me;
he refreshes my soul.

℟. **The Lord is my shepherd; there is nothing I shall want.**

Even though I walk in the dark valley
I fear no evil; for you are at my side
With your rod and your staff
that give me courage.

℟. **The Lord is my shepherd; there is nothing I shall want.**

You spread the table before me
in the sight of my foes;
You anoint my head with oil;
my cup overflows.

℟. **The Lord is my shepherd; there is nothing I shall want.**

Only goodness and kindness follow me
all the days of my life;
And I shall dwell in the house of the LORD
for years to come.

℟. **The Lord is my shepherd; there is nothing I shall want.**

ALLELUIA

John 10:14

℟. **Alleluia, alleluia.**

I am the good shepherd, says the Lord;
I know my sheep, and mine know me.

℟. **Alleluia, alleluia.**

GOSPEL

John 10:11-16 A good shepherd lays down his life for the sheep.

✠ **A reading from the holy Gospel according to John**

Jesus said:
"I am the good shepherd.
A good shepherd lays down his life for the sheep.
A hired man, who is not a shepherd
and whose sheep are not his own,
sees a wolf coming and leaves the sheep and runs away,
and the wolf catches and scatters them.
This is because he works for pay and has no concern for the sheep.
I am the good shepherd,
and I know mine and mine know me,
just as the Father knows me and I know the Father;
and I will lay down my life for the sheep.
I have other sheep that do not belong to this fold.
These also I must lead, and they will hear my voice,
and there will be one flock, one shepherd."

The Gospel of the Lord.

JULY 22

603 SAINT MARY MAGDALENE FEAST

FIRST READING

First Option

Song of Songs 3:1-4b I have found him whom my heart loves.

A reading from the Song of Songs

The Bride says:
On my bed at night I sought him
whom my heart loves—
I sought him but I did not find him.
I will rise then and go about the city;
in the streets and crossings I will seek
Him whom my heart loves.
I sought him but I did not find him.
The watchmen came upon me,
as they made their rounds of the city:
Have you seen him whom my heart loves?
I had hardly left them
when I found him whom my heart loves.

The word of the Lord.

OR:

Second Option

2 Corinthians 5:14-17 Even if we once knew Christ according to the flesh, yet now we know him so no longer.

A reading from the second Letter of Saint Paul to the Corinthians

Brothers and sisters:
The love of Christ impels us,
once we have come to the conviction that one died for all;
therefore, all have died.
He indeed died for all,
so that those who live might no longer live for themselves
but for him who for their sake died and was raised.

Consequently, from now on we regard no one according to the flesh;
even if we once knew Christ according to the flesh,
yet now we know him so no longer.
So whoever is in Christ is a new creation:
the old things have passed away;
behold, new things have come.

The word of the Lord.

RESPONSORIAL PSALM

Psalm 63:2, 3-4, 5-6, 8-9

℟. (2) **My soul is thirsting for you, O Lord my God.**

O God, you are my God whom I seek;
for you my flesh pines and my soul thirsts
like the earth, parched, lifeless and without water.

℟. **My soul is thirsting for you, O Lord my God.**

Thus have I gazed toward you in the sanctuary
to see your power and your glory,
For your kindness is a greater good than life;
my lips shall glorify you.

℟. **My soul is thirsting for you, O Lord my God.**

Thus will I bless you while I live;
lifting up my hands, I will call upon your name.
As with the riches of a banquet shall my soul be satisfied,
and with exultant lips my mouth shall praise you.

℟. **My soul is thirsting for you, O Lord my God.**

You are my help,
and in the shadow of your wings I shout for joy.
My soul clings fast to you;
your right hand upholds me.

℟. **My soul is thirsting for you, O Lord my God.**

ALLELUIA

℟. **Alleluia, alleluia.**

Tell us Mary, what did you see on the way?
I saw the glory of the risen Christ, I saw his empty tomb.

℟. **Alleluia, alleluia.**

GOSPEL

John 20:1-2, 11-18 Woman, why are you weeping? Whom are you looking for?

✠ **A reading from the holy Gospel according to John**

On the first day of the week,
Mary Magdalene came to the tomb early in the morning,
while it was still dark,
and saw the stone removed from the tomb.
So she ran and went to Simon Peter
and to the other disciple whom Jesus loved, and told them,
"They have taken the Lord from the tomb,
and we don't know where they put him."

Mary stayed outside the tomb weeping.
And as she wept, she bent over into the tomb
and saw two angels in white sitting there,
one at the head and one at the feet
where the body of Jesus had been.
And they said to her, "Woman, why are you weeping?"
She said to them, "They have taken my Lord,
and I don't know where they laid him."
When she had said this, she turned around and saw Jesus there,
but did not know it was Jesus.
Jesus said to her, "Woman, why are you weeping?
Whom are you looking for?"

She thought it was the gardener and said to him,
"Sir, if you carried him away,
tell me where you laid him,
and I will take him."
Jesus said to her, "Mary!"
She turned and said to him in Hebrew,
"Rabbouni," which means Teacher.
Jesus said to her,
"Stop holding on to me, for I have not yet ascended to the Father.
But go to my brothers and tell them,
'I am going to my Father and your Father,
to my God and your God.' "
Mary Magdalene went and announced to the disciples,
"I have seen the Lord,"
and then reported what he told her.

The Gospel of the Lord.

JULY 24

604A SAINT SHARBEL MAKHLŪF, PRIEST

From the Common of Pastors (vol. II, III, or IV, nos. 719–724), or the Common of Holy Men and Women (vol. II, III, or IV, nos. 737–742), or:

FIRST READING

Sirach 3:17-24 Humble yourself and you will find favor with God.

A reading from the Book of Sirach

My child, conduct your affairs with humility,
and you will be loved more than a giver of gifts.
Humble yourself the more, the greater you are,
and you will find favor with God.
The greater you are,
the more you must humble yourself in all things,
and you will find grace before God.
For great is the power of God;
by the humble he is glorified.
What is too sublime for you, seek not,
into things beyond your strength search not.
What is committed to you, attend to;
for it is not necessary for you to see with your eyes
those things which are hidden.
With what is too much for you meddle not,
when shown things beyond human understanding.
Their own opinion has misled many,
and false reasoning unbalanced their judgment.
Where the pupil of the eye is missing, there is no light,
and where there is no knowledge, there is no wisdom.

The word of the Lord.

RESPONSORIAL PSALM

Psalm 15:2-3ab, 3cd-4ab, 5

℟. (1) **The just one shall live on your holy mountain, O Lord.**

He who walks blamelessly and does justice;
who thinks the truth in his heart
and slanders not with his tongue.

℟. **The just one shall live on your holy mountain, O Lord.**

Who harms not his fellow man,
nor takes up a reproach against his neighbor;
By whom the reprobate is despised,
while he honors those who fear the LORD.

℟. **The just one shall live on your holy mountain, O Lord.**

Who lends not his money at usury
and accepts no bribe against the innocent.
He who does these things
shall never be disturbed.

℟. **The just one shall live on your holy mountain, O Lord.**

ALLELUIA

Matthew 5:3

℟. **Alleluia, alleluia.**

Blessed are the poor in spirit;
for theirs is the Kingdom of heaven.

℟. **Alleluia, alleluia.**

GOSPEL

Matthew 19:27-29 You who have followed me will receive a hundred times more.

✠ **A reading from the holy Gospel according to Matthew**

Peter said to Jesus,
"We have given up everything and followed you.
What will there be for us?"
Jesus said to them, "Amen, I say to you
that you who have followed me, in the new age,
when the Son of Man is seated on his throne of glory,
will yourselves sit on twelve thrones,
judging the twelve tribes of Israel.
And everyone who has given up houses or brothers or sisters
or father or mother or children or lands
for the sake of my name will receive a hundred times more,
and will inherit eternal life."

The Gospel of the Lord.

AUGUST 9

617A SAINT TERESA BENEDICTA OF THE CROSS, VIRGIN AND MARTYR

From the Common of Martyrs (vol. II, III, or IV, nos. 713–718), or the Common of Virgins (vol. II, III, or IV, nos. 731–736), or:

FIRST READING

Hosea 2:16bc, 17cd, 21-22 I will espouse you to me forever.

A reading from the Book of the Prophet Hosea

Thus says the LORD:
I will lead her into the desert
and speak to her heart.
She shall respond there as in the days of her youth,
when she came up from the land of Egypt.

I will espouse you to me forever:
I will espouse you in right and in justice,
in love and in mercy;
I will espouse you in fidelity,
and you shall know the LORD.

The word of the Lord.

RESPONSORIAL PSALM

Psalm 45:11-12, 14-15, 16-17

℟. (11) **Listen to me, daughter; see and bend your ear.**
or:
℟. **The bridegroom is here; let us go out to meet Christ the Lord.**

Hear, O daughter, and see; turn your ear,
forget your people and your father's house.
So shall the king desire your beauty;
for he is your lord, and you must worship him.

℟. **Listen to me, daughter; see and bend your ear.**
or:
℟. **The bridegroom is here; let us go out to meet Christ the Lord.**

All glorious is the king's daughter as she enters;
her raiment is threaded with spun gold.
In embroidered apparel she is borne in to the king;
behind her the virgins of her train are brought to you.

℟. **Listen to me, daughter; see and bend your ear.**
or:
℟. **The bridegroom is here; let us go out to meet Christ the Lord.**

They are borne in with gladness and joy;
they enter the palace of the king.
The place of your fathers your sons shall have;
you shall make them princes through all the land.

℟. **Listen to me, daughter; see and bend your ear.**
or:
℟. **The bridegroom is here; let us go out to meet Christ the Lord.**

ALLELUIA

℟. **Alleluia, alleluia.**

**Come, bride of Christ, and receive the crown,
which the Lord has prepared for you for ever.**

℟. **Alleluia, alleluia.**

GOSPEL

Matthew 25:1-13 Behold, the bridegroom! Come out to meet him!

✠ **A reading from the holy Gospel according to Matthew**

Jesus told his disciples this parable:
"The Kingdom of heaven will be like ten virgins
who took their lamps and went out to meet the bridegroom.
Five of them were foolish and five were wise.
The foolish ones, when taking their lamps,
brought no oil with them,
but the wise brought flasks of oil with their lamps.
Since the bridegroom was long delayed,
they all became drowsy and fell asleep.
At midnight, there was a cry,
'Behold, the bridegroom! Come out to meet him!'
Then all those virgins got up and trimmed their lamps.
The foolish ones said to the wise,
'Give us some of your oil,
for our lamps are going out.'
But the wise ones replied,
'No, for there may not be enough for us and you.
Go instead to the merchants and buy some for yourselves.'
While they went off to buy it,
the bridegroom came
and those who were ready went into the wedding feast with him.
Then the door was locked.
Afterwards the other virgins came and said,
'Lord, Lord, open the door for us!'
But he said in reply,
'Amen, I say to you, I do not know you.'
Therefore, stay awake,
for you know neither the day nor the hour."

The Gospel of the Lord.

AUGUST 12

623A SAINT JANE FRANCES DE CHANTAL, RELIGIOUS

Previously observed on August 18 in the United States, this Optional Memorial is transferred to this date in the General Roman Calendar.

From the Common of Holy Men and Women: For Religious (vol. II, III, or IV, nos. 737–742), or:

FIRST READING

Proverbs 31:10-13, 19-20, 30-31 The woman who fears the LORD is to be praised.

A reading from the Book of Proverbs

When one finds a worthy wife,
her value is far beyond pearls.
Her husband, entrusting his heart to her,
has an unfailing prize.
She brings him good, and not evil,
all the days of her life.
She obtains wool and flax
and makes cloth with skillful hands.
She puts her hands to the distaff,
and her fingers ply the spindle.
She reaches out her hands to the poor,
and extends her arms to the needy.
Charm is deceptive and beauty fleeting;
the woman who fears the LORD is to be praised.
Give her a reward of her labors,
and let her works praise her at the city gates.

The word of the Lord.

RESPONSORIAL PSALM

Psalm 131:1bcde, 2, 3

℟. **In you, Lord, I have found my peace.**

O Lord, my heart is not proud,
nor are my eyes haughty;
I busy not myself with great things,
nor with things too sublime for me.

℟. **In you, Lord, I have found my peace.**

Nay rather, I have stilled and quieted
my soul like a weaned child.
Like a weaned child on its mother's lap,
so is my soul within me.

℟. **In you, Lord, I have found my peace.**

O Israel, hope in the Lord,
both now and forever.

℟. **In you, Lord, I have found my peace.**

ALLELUIA

John 8:31b-32

℟. **Alleluia, alleluia.**

If you remain in my word, you will truly be my disciples,
and you will know the truth, says the Lord.

℟. **Alleluia, alleluia.**

GOSPEL

Mark 3:31-35 Whoever does the will of God is my brother and sister and mother.

✠ **A reading from the holy Gospel according to Mark**

The mother of Jesus and his brothers arrived.
Standing outside they sent word to him and called him.
A crowd seated around him told him,
"Your mother and your brothers and your sisters
are outside asking for you."
But he said to them in reply,
"Who are my mother and my brothers?"
And looking around at those seated in the circle he said,
"Here are my mother and my brothers.
For whoever does the will of God
is my brother and sister and mother."

The Gospel of the Lord.

SEPTEMBER 9

[In the Dioceses of the United States]

636A SAINT PETER CLAVER, PRIEST MEMORIAL

From the Common of Pastors (vol. II, III, or IV, nos. 719–724), or the Common of Holy Men and Women: For Those Who Work for the Underprivileged (vol. II, III, or IV, nos. 737–742), or:

FIRST READING

Isaiah 58:6-11 Share your bread with the hungry.

A reading from the Book of the Prophet Isaiah

Thus says the LORD:
This is the fasting that I wish:
releasing those bound unjustly,
untying the thongs of the yoke;
Setting free the oppressed,
breaking every yoke;
Sharing your bread with the hungry,
sheltering the oppressed and the homeless;
Clothing the naked when you see them,
and not turning your back on your own.
Then your light shall break forth like the dawn,
and your wound shall quickly be healed;
Your vindication shall go before you,
and the glory of the LORD shall be your rear guard.
Then you shall call, and the LORD will answer,
you shall cry for help, and he will say: Here I am!
If you remove from your midst oppression,
false accusation and malicious speech;
If you bestow your bread on the hungry
and satisfy the afflicted;

Then light shall rise for you in darkness,
and the gloom shall become for you like midday;
Then the LORD will guide you always
and give you plenty even on the parched land.
He will renew your strength,
and you shall be like a watered garden,
like a spring whose water never fails.

The word of the Lord.

RESPONSORIAL PSALM

Psalm 1:1-2, 3, 4 and 6

℟. (40:5a) **Blessed are they who hope in the Lord.**

or:

℟. (2a) **Blessed are they who delight in the law of the Lord.**

or:

℟. (92:13-14) **The just will flourish like the palm tree in the garden of the Lord.**

Blessed the man who follows not
the counsel of the wicked
Nor walks in the way of sinners,
nor sits in the company of the insolent,
But delights in the law of the LORD
and meditates on his law day and night.

℟. **Blessed are they who hope in the Lord.**

or:

℟. **Blessed are they who delight in the law of the Lord.**

or:

℟. **The just will flourish like the palm tree in the garden of the Lord.**

He is like a tree
planted near running water,
That yields its fruit in due season,
and whose leaves never fade.
Whatever he does, prospers.

℟. **Blessed are they who hope in the Lord.**

or:

℟. **Blessed are they who delight in the law of the Lord.**

or:

℟. **The just will flourish like the palm tree in the garden of the Lord.**

Not so, the wicked, not so;
they are like chaff which the wind drives away.
For the LORD watches over the way of the just,
but the way of the wicked vanishes.

℟. **Blessed are they who hope in the Lord.**

or:

℟. **Blessed are they who delight in the law of the Lord.**

or:

℟. **The just will flourish like the palm tree in the garden of the Lord.**

ALLELUIA

John 13:34

℟. **Alleluia, alleluia.**

I give you a new commandment:
love one another as I have loved you.

℟. **Alleluia, alleluia.**

GOSPEL

Matthew 25:31-40 Whatever you did for the least of my brothers, you did for me.

✠ **A reading from the holy Gospel according to Matthew**

Jesus said to his disciples:
"When the Son of Man comes in his glory,
and all the angels with him,
he will sit upon his glorious throne,
and all the nations will be assembled before him.
And he will separate them one from another,
as a shepherd separates the sheep from the goats.
He will place the sheep on his right and the goats on his left.
Then the king will say to those on his right,
'Come, you who are blessed by my Father.
Inherit the kingdom prepared for you from the foundation of the world.
For I was hungry and you gave me food,
I was thirsty and you gave me drink,
a stranger and you welcomed me,
naked and you clothed me,
ill and you cared for me,
in prison and you visited me.'
Then the righteous will answer him and say,
'Lord, when did we see you hungry and feed you,
or thirsty and give you drink?
When did we see you a stranger and welcome you,
or naked and clothe you?
When did we see you ill or in prison, and visit you?'
And the king will say to them in reply,
'Amen, I say to you, whatever you did
for one of the least brothers of mine you did for me.' "

The Gospel of the Lord.

SEPTEMBER 12

636B THE MOST HOLY NAME OF MARY

From the Common of the Blessed Virgin Mary (vol. II, III, or IV, nos. 707–712), or:

FIRST READING

Galatians 4:4-7 God sent his Son, born of a woman.

A reading from the Letter of Saint Paul to the Galatians

Brothers and sisters:
When the fullness of time had come, God sent his Son,
born of a woman, born under the law,
to ransom those under the law,
so that we might receive adoption as sons.
As proof that you are sons,
God sent the spirit of his Son into our hearts,
crying out, "Abba, Father!"
So you are no longer a slave but a son,
and if a son then also an heir, through God.

The word of the Lord.

RESPONSORIAL PSALM

Luke 1:46-47, 48-49, 50-51, 52-53, 54-55

℟. (49) **The Almighty has done great things for me, and holy is his Name.**

or:

℟. **O Blessed Virgin Mary, you carried the Son of the eternal Father.**

"My soul proclaims the greatness of the Lord,
my spirit rejoices in God my Savior."

℟. **The Almighty has done great things for me, and holy is his Name.**

or:

℟. **O Blessed Virgin Mary, you carried the Son of the eternal Father.**

"For he has looked with favor on his lowly servant.
From this day all generations will call me blessed:
the Almighty has done great things for me
and holy is his Name."

℟. **The Almighty has done great things for me, and holy is his Name.**

or:

℟. **O Blessed Virgin Mary, you carried the Son of the eternal Father.**

"He has mercy on those who fear him
in every generation.
He has shown the strength of his arm,
he has scattered the proud in their conceit."

℟. **The Almighty has done great things for me, and holy is his Name.**

or:

℟. **O Blessed Virgin Mary, you carried the Son of the eternal Father.**

"He has cast down the mighty from their thrones,
and has lifted up the lowly.
He has filled the hungry with good things,
and the rich he has sent away empty."

℟. **The Almighty has done great things for me, and holy is his Name.**

or:

℟. **O Blessed Virgin Mary, you carried the Son of the eternal Father.**

"He has come to the help of his servant Israel
for he has remembered his promise of mercy,
the promise he made to our fathers,
to Abraham and his children for ever."

℟. **The Almighty has done great things for me, and holy is his Name.**

or:

℟. **O Blessed Virgin Mary, you carried the Son of the eternal Father.**

ALLELUIA

See Luke 1:45

℟. **Alleluia, alleluia.**

Blessed are you, O Virgin Mary, who believed
that what was spoken to you by the Lord would be fulfilled.

℟. **Alleluia, alleluia.**

GOSPEL

Luke 1:39-47 Blessed is she who believed.

✠ **A reading from the holy Gospel according to Luke**

Mary set out
and traveled to the hill country in haste
to a town of Judah,
where she entered the house of Zechariah
and greeted Elizabeth.
When Elizabeth heard Mary's greeting,
the infant leaped in her womb,
and Elizabeth, filled with the Holy Spirit,
cried out in a loud voice and said,
"Most blessed are you among women,
and blessed is the fruit of your womb.
And how does this happen to me,
that the mother of my Lord should come to me?
For at the moment the sound of your greeting reached my ears,
the infant in my womb leaped for joy.
Blessed are you who believed
that what was spoken to you by the Lord
would be fulfilled."

And Mary said:

"My soul proclaims the greatness of the Lord;
my spirit rejoices in God my savior."

The Gospel of the Lord.

SEPTEMBER 23

643A SAINT PIUS OF PIETRELCINA, PRIEST
MEMORIAL

From the Common of Pastors (vol. II, III, or IV, nos. 719–724), or the Common of Holy Men and Women: For Religious (vol. II, III, or IV, nos. 737–742), or:

FIRST READING

Galatians 2:19-20 I live, no longer I, but Christ lives in me.

A reading from the Letter of Saint Paul to the Galatians

Brothers and sisters:
Through the law I died to the law,
that I might live for God.
I have been crucified with Christ;
yet I live, no longer I, but Christ lives in me;
insofar as I now live in the flesh,
I live by faith in the Son of God
who has loved me and given himself up for me.

The word of the Lord.

RESPONSORIAL PSALM

Psalm 128:1-2, 3, 4-5

℟. (1) **Blessed are those who fear the Lord.**

Blessed are you who fear the LORD,
who walk in his ways!
For you shall eat the fruit of your handiwork;
blessed shall you be, and favored.

℟. **Blessed are those who fear the Lord.**

Your wife shall be like a fruitful vine
in the recesses of your home;
Your children like olive plants
around your table.

℟. **Blessed are those who fear the Lord.**

Behold, thus is the man blessed
who fears the LORD.
The LORD bless you from Zion:
may you see the prosperity of Jerusalem
all the days of your life.

℟. **Blessed are those who fear the Lord.**

ALLELUIA

Luke 21:36

℟. **Alleluia, alleluia.**

Be vigilant at all times
and pray that you may have the strength to stand before the Son of Man.

℟. **Alleluia, alleluia.**

GOSPEL

Matthew 16:24-27 Whoever loses his life for my sake will find it.

✠ **A reading from the holy Gospel according to Matthew**

Jesus said to his disciples,
"Whoever wishes to come after me must deny himself,
take up his cross, and follow me.
For whoever wishes to save his life will lose it,
but whoever loses his life for my sake will find it.
What profit would there be for one to gain the whole world
and forfeit his life?
Or what can one give in exchange for his life?
For the Son of Man will come with his angels in his Father's glory,
and then he will repay each one according to his conduct."

The Gospel of the Lord.

SEPTEMBER 28

645A SAINT LAWRENCE RUIZ AND COMPANIONS, MARTYRS

From the Common of Martyrs (vol. II, III, or IV, nos. 713–718), or:

FIRST READING

2 Maccabees 7:1-2, 9-14 We are ready to die rather than transgress the laws of our ancestors.

A reading from the second Book of Maccabees

It happened that seven brothers with their mother were arrested
and tortured with whips and scourges by the king,
to force them to eat pork in violation of God's law.
One of the brothers, speaking for the others, said:
"What do you expect to achieve by questioning us?
We are ready to die rather than transgress the laws of our ancestors."

At the point of death, the second brother said:
"You accursed fiend, you are depriving us of this present life,
but the King of the world will raise us up to live again forever.
It is for his laws that we are dying."

After him the third suffered their cruel sport.
He put out his tongue at once when told to do so,
and bravely held out his hands, as he spoke these noble words:
"It was from Heaven that I received these;
for the sake of his laws I disdain them;
from him I hope to receive them again."
Even the king and his attendants marveled at the young man's courage,
because he regarded his sufferings as nothing.

After he had died,
they tortured and maltreated the fourth brother in the same way.
When he was near death, he said,
"It is my choice to die at the hands of men
with the hope God gives of being raised up by him;
but for you, there will be no resurrection to life."

The word of the Lord.

RESPONSORIAL PSALM

Psalm 34:2-3, 4-5, 6-7, 8-9

℟. (5) **The Lord delivered me from all my fears.**

I will bless the LORD at all times;
his praise shall be ever in my mouth.
Let my soul glory in the LORD;
the lowly will hear me and be glad.

℟. **The Lord delivered me from all my fears.**

Glorify the LORD with me,
let us together extol his name.
I sought the LORD, and he answered me
and delivered me from all my fears.

℟. **The Lord delivered me from all my fears.**

Look to him that you may be radiant with joy,
and your faces may not blush with shame.
When the afflicted man called out, the LORD heard,
and from all his distress he saved him.

℟. **The Lord delivered me from all my fears.**

The angel of the LORD encamps
around those who fear him, and delivers them.
Taste and see how good the LORD is;
blessed the man who takes refuge in him.

℟. **The Lord delivered me from all my fears.**

ALLELUIA

Matthew 5:10

℟. **Alleluia, alleluia.**

**Blessed are they who are persecuted for the sake of righteousness,
for theirs is the Kingdom of heaven.**

℟. **Alleluia, alleluia.**

GOSPEL

John 15:18-21 If they persecuted me, they will also persecute you.

✠ **A reading from the holy Gospel according to John**

**Jesus said to his disciples:
"If the world hates you, realize that it hated me first.
If you belonged to the world, the world would love its own;
but because you do not belong to the world,
and I have chosen you out of the world,
the world hates you.
Remember the word I spoke to you,
'No slave is greater than his master.'
If they persecuted me, they will also persecute you.
If they kept my word, they will also keep yours.
And they will do all these things to you on account of my name,
because they do not know the one who sent me."**

The Gospel of the Lord.

OCTOBER 5

[In the Dioceses of the United States]

651A BLESSED FRANCIS XAVIER SEELOS, PRIEST

From the Common of Pastors: For Missionaries (vol. II, III, or IV, nos. 719–724).

OCTOBER 11

655A SAINT JOHN XXIII, POPE

From the Common of Pastors: For a Pope (vol. II, III, or IV, nos. 719–724), or:

FIRST READING

Ezekiel 34:11-16 As a shepherd tends his flock, so will I tend my sheep.

A reading from the Book of the Prophet Ezekiel

Thus says the Lord God:
I myself will look after and tend my sheep.
As a shepherd tends his flock
when he finds himself among his scattered sheep,
so will I tend my sheep.
I will rescue them from every place where they were scattered
when it was cloudy and dark.
I will lead them out from among the peoples
and gather them from the foreign lands;
I will bring them back to their own country
and pasture them upon the mountains of Israel
in the land's ravines and all its inhabited places.
In good pastures will I pasture them,
and on the mountain heights of Israel
shall be their grazing ground.
There they shall lie down on good grazing ground,
and in rich pastures shall they be pastured
on the mountains of Israel.
I myself will pasture my sheep;
I myself will give them rest, says the Lord God.
The lost I will seek out,
the strayed I will bring back,

the injured I will bind up,
the sick I will heal,
but the sleek and the strong I will destroy,
shepherding them rightly.

The word of the Lord.

RESPONSORIAL PSALM

Psalm 23:1-3a, 4, 5, 6

℟. (1) **The Lord is my shepherd; there is nothing I shall want.**

The Lord is my shepherd; I shall not want.
In verdant pastures he gives me repose;
Beside restful waters he leads me;
he refreshes my soul.

℟. **The Lord is my shepherd; there is nothing I shall want.**

Even though I walk in the dark valley
I fear no evil; for you are at my side
With your rod and your staff
that give me courage.

℟. **The Lord is my shepherd; there is nothing I shall want.**

You spread the table before me
in the sight of my foes;
You anoint my head with oil;
my cup overflows.

℟. **The Lord is my shepherd; there is nothing I shall want.**

Only goodness and kindness follow me
all the days of my life;
And I shall dwell in the house of the Lord
for years to come.

℟. **The Lord is my shepherd; there is nothing I shall want.**

ALLELUIA

John 10:14

℟. **Alleluia, alleluia.**

I am the good shepherd, says the Lord;
I know my sheep, and mine know me.

℟. **Alleluia, alleluia.**

GOSPEL

John 21:15-17 Feed my lambs, feed my sheep.

✠ **A reading from the holy Gospel according to John**

After Jesus had revealed himself to his disciples and
eaten breakfast with them, he said to Simon Peter,
"Simon, son of John, do you love me more than these?"
Simon Peter answered him, "Yes, Lord, you know that I love you."
Jesus said to him, "Feed my lambs."
He then said to Simon Peter a second time,
"Simon, son of John, do you love me?"
Simon Peter answered him, "Yes, Lord, you know that I love you."
He said to him, "Tend my sheep."
He said to him the third time,
"Simon, son of John, do you love me?"
Peter was distressed that he had said to him a third time,
"Do you love me?" and he said to him,
"Lord, you know everything; you know that I love you."
Jesus said to him, "Feed my sheep."

The Gospel of the Lord.

OCTOBER 22

663A SAINT JOHN PAUL II, POPE

From the Common of Pastors: For a Pope (vol. II, III, or IV, nos. 719–724), or:

FIRST READING

Isaiah 52:7-10 All the ends of the earth will behold the salvation of our God.

A reading from the Book of the Prophet Isaiah

How beautiful upon the mountains
are the feet of him who brings glad tidings,
Announcing peace, bearing good news,
announcing salvation, and saying to Zion,
"Your God is King!"
Hark! Your sentinels raise a cry,
together they shout for joy,
For they see directly, before their eyes,
the LORD restoring Zion.
Break out together in song,
O ruins of Jerusalem!
For the LORD comforts his people,
he redeems Jerusalem.
The LORD has bared his holy arm
in the sight of all the nations;
All the ends of the earth will behold
the salvation of our God.

The word of the Lord.

RESPONSORIAL PSALM

Psalm 96:1-2a, 2b-3, 7-8a, 10

℟. (3) **Proclaim God's marvelous deeds to all the nations.**

Sing to the LORD a new song;
sing to the LORD, all you lands.
Sing to the LORD; bless his name.

℟. **Proclaim God's marvelous deeds to all the nations.**

Announce his salvation, day after day.
Tell his glory among the nations;
among all peoples, his wondrous deeds.

℟. **Proclaim God's marvelous deeds to all the nations.**

Give to the LORD, you families of nations,
give to the LORD glory and praise;
give to the LORD the glory due his name!

℟. **Proclaim God's marvelous deeds to all the nations.**

Say among the nations: The LORD is king.
He has made the world firm, not to be moved;
he governs the peoples with equity.

℟. **Proclaim God's marvelous deeds to all the nations.**

ALLELUIA

John 10:14

℟. **Alleluia, alleluia.**

I am the good shepherd, says the Lord;
I know my sheep, and mine know me.

℟. **Alleluia, alleluia.**

GOSPEL

John 21:15-17 Feed my lambs, feed my sheep.

✠ **A reading from the holy Gospel according to John**

After Jesus had revealed himself to his disciples and
eaten breakfast with them, he said to Simon Peter,
"Simon, son of John, do you love me more than these?"
Simon Peter answered him, "Yes, Lord, you know that I love you."
Jesus said to him, "Feed my lambs."
He then said to Simon Peter a second time,
"Simon, son of John, do you love me?"
Simon Peter answered him, "Yes, Lord, you know that I love you."
He said to him, "Tend my sheep."
He said to him the third time,
"Simon, son of John, do you love me?"
Peter was distressed that he had said to him a third time,
"Do you love me?" and he said to him,
"Lord, you know everything; you know that I love you."
Jesus said to him, "Feed my sheep."

The Gospel of the Lord.

NOVEMBER 24

683B SAINT ANDREW DŨNG-LẠC, PRIEST, AND COMPANIONS, MARTYRS MEMORIAL

From the Common of Martyrs (vol. II, III, or IV, nos. 713–718), or:

FIRST READING

Wisdom 3:1-9 As sacrificial offerings he took them to himself.

A reading from the Book of Wisdom

The souls of the just are in the hand of God,
and no torment shall touch them.
They seemed, in the view of the foolish, to be dead;
and their passing away was thought an affliction
and their going forth from us, utter destruction.
But they are in peace.
For if before men, indeed, they be punished,
yet is their hope full of immortality;
Chastised a little, they shall be greatly blessed,
because God tried them
and found them worthy of himself.
As gold in the furnace, he proved them,
and as sacrificial offerings he took them to himself.
In the time of their visitation they shall shine,
and shall dart about as sparks through stubble;
They shall judge nations and rule over peoples,
and the LORD shall be their King forever.
Those who trust in him shall understand truth,
and the faithful shall abide with him in love:
Because grace and mercy are with his holy ones,
and his care is with his elect.

The word of the Lord.

RESPONSORIAL PSALM

Psalm 126:1-2ab, 2cd-3, 4-5, 6

℟. (5) **Those who sow in tears shall reap rejoicing.**

When the LORD brought back the captives of Zion,
we were like men dreaming.
Then our mouth was filled with laughter,
and our tongue with rejoicing.

℟. **Those who sow in tears shall reap rejoicing.**

Then they said among the nations,
"The LORD has done great things for them."
The LORD has done great things for us;
we are glad indeed.

℟. **Those who sow in tears shall reap rejoicing.**

Restore our fortunes, O LORD,
like the torrents in the southern desert.
Those who sow in tears
shall reap rejoicing.

℟. **Those who sow in tears shall reap rejoicing.**

Although they go forth weeping,
carrying the seed to be sown,
They shall come back rejoicing,
carrying their sheaves.

℟. **Those who sow in tears shall reap rejoicing.**

ALLELUIA

1 Peter 4:14

℟. **Alleluia, alleluia.**

If you are insulted for the name of Christ, blessed are you,
for the Spirit of God rests upon you.

℟. **Alleluia, alleluia.**

GOSPEL

Matthew 10:17-22 You will be led before governors and kings for my sake, as a witness before them and the pagans.

✠ **A reading from the holy Gospel according to Matthew**

Jesus said to his Apostles:
“Beware of men, for they will hand you over to courts
and scourge you in their synagogues,
and you will be led before governors and kings for my sake
as a witness before them and the pagans.
When they hand you over,
do not worry about how you are to speak
or what you are to say.
You will be given at that moment what you are to say.
For it will not be you who speak
but the Spirit of your Father speaking through you.
Brother will hand over brother to death,
and the father his child;
children will rise up against parents and have them put to death.
You will be hated by all because of my name,
but whoever endures to the end will be saved.”

The Gospel of the Lord.

NOVEMBER 25

683C SAINT CATHERINE OF ALEXANDRIA, VIRGIN AND MARTYR

From the Common of Martyrs (vol. II, III, or IV, nos. 713–718), or the Common of Virgins (vol. II, III, or IV, nos. 731–736), or:

FIRST READING

Revelation 21:5-7 The victor will inherit these gifts.

A reading from the Book of Revelation

The One who was seated on the throne said:
"Behold, I make all things new."
Then he said, "Write these words down,
for they are trustworthy and true."
He said to me, "They are accomplished.
I am the Alpha and the Omega, the beginning and the end.
To the thirsty I will give a gift
from the spring of life-giving water.
The victor will inherit these gifts,
and I shall be his God,
and he will be my son."

The word of the Lord.

RESPONSORIAL PSALM

Psalm 124:2-3, 4-5, 7cd-8

℟. (7) **Our soul has been rescued like a bird from the fowler's snare.**

Had not the LORD been with us–
When men rose up against us,
then would they have swallowed us alive
When their fury was inflamed against us.

℟. **Our soul has been rescued like a bird from the fowler's snare.**

Then would the waters have overwhelmed us;
The torrent would have swept over us;
over us then would have swept
the raging waters.

℟. **Our soul has been rescued like a bird from the fowler's snare.**

Broken was the snare,
and we were freed.
Our help is in the name of the LORD,
who made heaven and earth.

℟. **Our soul has been rescued like a bird from the fowler's snare.**

ALLELUIA

See *Te Deum*

℟. **Alleluia, alleluia.**

We praise you, O God,
we acclaim you as Lord;
the white-robed army of martyrs praises you.

℟. **Alleluia, alleluia.**

GOSPEL

Matthew 10:28-33 Do not be afraid of those who kill the body.

✠ **A reading from the holy Gospel according to Matthew**

Jesus said to his Apostles:
"Do not be afraid of those who kill the body
but cannot kill the soul;
rather, be afraid of the one who can destroy
both soul and body in Gehenna.
Are not two sparrows sold for a small coin?
Yet not one of them falls to the ground without your Father's knowledge.
Even all the hairs of your head are counted.
So do not be afraid; you are worth more than many sparrows.
Everyone who acknowledges me before others
I will acknowledge before my heavenly Father.
But whoever denies me before others,
I will deny before my heavenly Father."

The Gospel of the Lord.

DECEMBER 9

689A SAINT JUAN DIEGO CUAUHTLATOATZIN

From the Common of Holy Men and Women (vol. II, III, or IV, nos. 737–742), or:

FIRST READING

1 Corinthians 1:26-31 God chose the weak of the world.

A reading from the first Letter of Saint Paul to the Corinthians

Consider your own calling, brothers and sisters.
Not many of you were wise by human standards,
not many were powerful,
not many were of noble birth.
Rather, God chose the foolish of the world to shame the wise,
and God chose the weak of the world to shame the strong,
and God chose the lowly and despised of the world,
those who count for nothing,
to reduce to nothing those who are something,
so that no human being might boast before God.
It is due to him that you are in Christ Jesus,
who became for us wisdom from God,
as well as righteousness, sanctification, and redemption,
so that, as it is written,
Whoever boasts, should boast in the Lord.

The word of the Lord.

RESPONSORIAL PSALM

Psalm 131:1bcde, 2, 3

℟. **In you, Lord, I have found my peace.**

O LORD, my heart is not proud,
nor are my eyes haughty;
I busy not myself with great things,
nor with things too sublime for me.

℟. **In you, Lord, I have found my peace.**

Nay rather, I have stilled and quieted
my soul like a weaned child.
Like a weaned child on its mother's lap,
so is my soul within me.

℟. **In you, Lord, I have found my peace.**

O Israel, hope in the LORD,
both now and forever.

℟. **In you, Lord, I have found my peace.**

ALLELUIA

See Matthew 11:25

℟. **Alleluia, alleluia.**

Blessed are you, Father, Lord of heaven and earth;
you have revealed to little ones the mysteries of the Kingdom.

℟. **Alleluia, alleluia.**

GOSPEL

Matthew 11:25-30 Although you have hidden these things from the wise and the learned, you have revealed them to the childlike.

✠ **A reading from the holy Gospel according to Matthew**

At that time Jesus exclaimed:
"I give praise to you, Father, Lord of heaven and earth,
for although you have hidden these things
from the wise and the learned
you have revealed them to the childlike.
Yes, Father, such has been your gracious will.
All things have been handed over to me by my Father.
No one knows the Son except the Father,
and no one knows the Father except the Son
and anyone to whom the Son wishes to reveal him.

"Come to me, all you who labor and are burdened,
and I will give you rest.
Take my yoke upon you and learn from me,
for I am meek and humble of heart;
and you will find rest for yourselves.
For my yoke is easy, and my burden light."

The Gospel of the Lord.

RITUAL MASSES

VI. FOR THE CONFERRAL OF THE SACRAMENT OF MARRIAGE

802 READING FROM THE NEW TESTAMENT

5A.*

Ephesians 4:1-6 One Body and one Spirit.

A reading from the Letter of Saint Paul to the Ephesians

Brothers and sisters:
I, a prisoner for the Lord,
urge you to live in a manner worthy of the call you have received,
with all humility and gentleness, with patience,
bearing with one another through love,
striving to preserve the unity of the Spirit
through the bond of peace: one Body and one Spirit,
as you were also called to the one hope of your call;
one Lord, one faith, one baptism;
one God and Father of all,
who is over all and through all and in all.

The word of the Lord.

---

* For New Testament reading options 1–13, see vol. IV, no. 802.

MASSES FOR VARIOUS NEEDS AND OCCASIONS

III. IN VARIOUS PUBLIC CIRCUMSTANCES

[In the Dioceses of the United States]

26A. FOR GIVING THANKS TO GOD FOR THE GIFT OF HUMAN LIFE

947A READING FROM THE OLD TESTAMENT

First Option

Genesis 1:1–2:2 God looked at everything he had made, and he found it very good.

A reading from the Book of Genesis

In the beginning, when God created the heavens and the earth,
the earth was a formless wasteland, and darkness covered the abyss,
while a mighty wind swept over the waters.

Then God said,
"Let there be light," and there was light.
God saw how good the light was.
God then separated the light from the darkness.
God called the light "day," and the darkness he called "night."
Thus evening came, and morning followed—the first day.

Then God said,
"Let there be a dome in the middle of the waters,
to separate one body of water from the other."
And so it happened:
God made the dome,
and it separated the water above the dome from the water below it.
God called the dome "the sky."
Evening came, and morning followed—the second day.

Then God said,
"Let the water under the sky be gathered into a single basin,
so that the dry land may appear."
And so it happened:
the water under the sky was gathered into its basin,
and the dry land appeared.
God called the dry land "the earth,"
and the basin of the water he called "the sea."
God saw how good it was.
Then God said,
"Let the earth bring forth vegetation:
every kind of plant that bears seed
and every kind of fruit tree on earth
that bears fruit with its seed in it."
And so it happened:
the earth brought forth every kind of plant that bears seed
and every kind of fruit tree on earth
that bears fruit with its seed in it.
God saw how good it was.
Evening came, and morning followed—the third day.

Then God said:
"Let there be lights in the dome of the sky,
to separate day from night.
Let them mark the fixed times, the days and the years,
and serve as luminaries in the dome of the sky,
to shed light upon the earth."
And so it happened:
God made the two great lights,
the greater one to govern the day,
and the lesser one to govern the night;
and he made the stars.

God set them in the dome of the sky,
to shed light upon the earth,
to govern the day and the night,
and to separate the light from the darkness.
God saw how good it was.
Evening came, and morning followed—the fourth day.

Then God said,
"Let the water teem with an abundance of living creatures,
and on the earth let birds fly beneath the dome of the sky."
And so it happened:
God created the great sea monsters
and all kinds of swimming creatures with which the
water teems,
and all kinds of winged birds.
God saw how good it was, and God blessed them, saying,
"Be fertile, multiply, and fill the water of the seas;
and let the birds multiply on the earth."
Evening came, and morning followed—the fifth day.

Then God said,
"Let the earth bring forth all kinds of living creatures:
cattle, creeping things, and wild animals of all kinds."
And so it happened:
God made all kinds of wild animals, all kinds of cattle,
and all kinds of creeping things of the earth.
God saw how good it was.

Then God said:
"Let us make man in our image, after our likeness.
Let them have dominion over the fish of the sea,
the birds of the air, and the cattle,
and over all the wild animals
and all the creatures that crawl on the ground."

God created man in his image;
in the image of God he created him;
male and female he created them.
God blessed them, saying:
"Be fertile and multiply;
fill the earth and subdue it.
Have dominion over the fish of the sea, the birds of the air,
and all the living things that move on the earth."
God also said:
"See, I give you every seed-bearing plant all over the earth
and every tree that has seed-bearing fruit on it to be your food;
and to all the animals of the land, all the birds of the air,
and all the living creatures that crawl on the ground,
I give all the green plants for food."
And so it happened.
God looked at everything he had made, and he found it very good.
Evening came, and morning followed—the sixth day.

Thus the heavens and the earth and all their array were completed.
Since on the seventh day God was finished
with the work he had been doing,
he rested on the seventh day from all the work he had undertaken.

The word of the Lord.

Second Option

2 Maccabees 7:1, 20-31 The creator of the universe will give you back both breath and life.

A reading from the second Book of Maccabees

It happened that seven brothers with their mother were arrested
and tortured with whips and scourges by the king,
to force them to eat pork in violation of God's law.

Most admirable and worthy of everlasting remembrance was the mother,
who saw her seven sons perish in a single day,
yet bore it courageously because of her hope in the Lord.
Filled with a noble spirit that stirred her womanly heart with manly courage,
she exhorted each of them
in the language of their forefathers with these words:
"I do not know how you came into existence in my womb;
it was not I who gave you the breath of life,
nor was it I who set in order
the elements of which each of you is composed.
Therefore, since it is the Creator of the universe
who shapes each man's beginning,
as he brings about the origin of everything,
he, in his mercy,
will give you back both breath and life,
because you now disregard yourselves for the sake of his law."

Antiochus, suspecting insult in her words,
thought he was being ridiculed.
As the youngest brother was still alive, the king appealed to him,
not with mere words, but with promises on oath,
to make him rich and happy if he would abandon his ancestral customs:

he would make him his Friend
and entrust him with high office.
When the youth paid no attention to him at all,
the king appealed to the mother,
urging her to advise her boy to save his life.
After he had urged her for a long time,
she went through the motions of persuading her son.
In derision of the cruel tyrant,
she leaned over close to her son and said in their native language:
"Son, have pity on me, who carried you in my womb for nine months,
nursed you for three years, brought you up,
educated and supported you to your present age.
I beg you, child, to look at the heavens and the earth
and see all that is in them;
then you will know that God did not make them out of existing things;
and in the same way the human race came into existence.
Do not be afraid of this executioner,
but be worthy of your brothers and accept death,
so that in the time of mercy I may receive you again with them."

She had scarcely finished speaking when the youth said:
"What are you waiting for?
I will not obey the king's command.
I obey the command of the law given to our fathers through Moses.
But you, who have contrived every kind of affliction for the Hebrews,
will not escape the hands of God."

The word of the Lord.

Third Option

Isaiah 49:1-6 I will make you a light to the nations.

A reading from the Book of the Prophet Isaiah

Hear me, O coastlands,
listen, O distant peoples.
The Lord called me from birth,
from my mother's womb he gave me my name.
He made of me a sharp-edged sword
and concealed me in the shadow of his arm.
He made me a polished arrow,
in his quiver he hid me.
You are my servant, he said to me,
Israel, through whom I show my glory.

Though I thought I had toiled in vain,
and for nothing, uselessly, spent my strength,
Yet my reward is with the Lord,
my recompense is with my God.
For now the Lord has spoken
who formed me as his servant from the womb,
that Jacob may be brought back to him
and Israel gathered to him;
and I am made glorious in the sight of the Lord,
and my God is now my strength!
It is too little, he says, for you to be my servant,
to raise up the tribes of Jacob,
and restore the survivors of Israel;
I will make you a light to the nations,
that my salvation may reach to the ends of the earth.

The word of the Lord.

947B READING FROM THE NEW TESTAMENT

First Option

Romans 11:33-36 From God and through him and for him are all things.

A reading from the Letter of Saint Paul to the Romans

Oh, the depth of the riches and wisdom and knowledge of God!
How inscrutable are his judgments and how unsearchable
his ways!
For who has known the mind of the Lord
or who has been his counselor?
Or who has given him anything
that he may be repaid?
For from him and through him and for him are all things.
To him be glory forever. Amen.

The word of the Lord.

Second Option

Ephesians 1:3-14 God chose us in Christ, before the foundation of the world.

A reading from the Letter of Saint Paul to the Ephesians

Blessed be the God and Father of our Lord Jesus Christ,
who has blessed us in Christ
with every spiritual blessing in the heavens,
as he chose us in him, before the foundation of the world,
to be holy and without blemish before him.
In love he destined us for adoption to himself through Jesus Christ,
in accord with the favor of his will,
for the praise of the glory of his grace
that he granted us in the beloved.

In him we have redemption by his Blood,
the forgiveness of transgressions,
in accord with the riches of his grace that he lavished upon us.
In all wisdom and insight, he has made known to us
the mystery of his will in accord with his favor
that he set forth in him as a plan for the fullness of times,
to sum up all things in Christ, in heaven and on earth.

In him we were also chosen,
destined in accord with the purpose of the One
who accomplishes all things according to the intention of his will,
so that we might exist for the praise of his glory,
we who first hoped in Christ.
In him you also, who have heard the word of truth,
the gospel of your salvation, and have believed in him,
were sealed with the promised Holy Spirit,
which is the first installment of our inheritance
toward redemption as God's possession, to the praise of his glory.

The word of the Lord.

Third Option

Ephesians 3:14-21 Rooted and grounded in love, you may be filled with the fullness of God.

A reading from the Letter of Saint Paul to the Ephesians

Brothers and sisters:
I kneel before the Father,
from whom every family in heaven and on earth is named,
that he may grant you in accord with the riches of his glory
to be strengthened with power through his Spirit in the inner self,
and that Christ may dwell in your hearts through faith;
that you, rooted and grounded in love,
may have strength to comprehend with all the holy ones
what is the breadth and length and height and depth,
and to know the love of Christ that surpasses knowledge,
so that you may be filled with all the fullness of God.

Now to him who is able to accomplish far more than all we ask or imagine,
by the power at work within us,
to him be glory in the Church and in Christ Jesus
to all generations, forever and ever. Amen.

The word of the Lord.

Fourth Option

Colossians 1:12-20 He transferred us to the kingdom of his beloved Son.

A reading from the Letter of Saint Paul to the Colossians

Brothers and sisters:
Let us give thanks to the Father,
who has made you fit to share
in the inheritance of the holy ones in light.
He delivered us from the power of darkness
and transferred us to the kingdom of his beloved Son,
in whom we have redemption, the forgiveness of sins.

He is the image of the invisible God,
the firstborn of all creation.
For in him were created all things in heaven and on earth,
the visible and the invisible,
whether thrones or dominions or principalities or powers;
all things were created through him and for him.
He is beforc all things,
and in him all things hold together.
He is the head of the body, the church.
He is the beginning, the firstborn from the dead,
that in all things he himself might be preeminent.
For in him all the fullness was pleased to dwell,
and through him to reconcile all things for him,
making peace by the blood of his cross
through him, whether those on earth or those in heaven.

The word of the Lord.

Fifth Option

1 John 3:11-21 We have passed from death to life because we love our brothers.

A reading from the first Letter of Saint John

Beloved:
This is the message you have heard from the beginning:
we should love one another,
unlike Cain who belonged to the Evil One
and slaughtered his brother.
Why did he slaughter him?
Because his own works were evil,
and those of his brother righteous.
Do not be amazed, then, brothers and sisters, if the world hates you.
We know that we have passed from death to life
because we love our brothers.
Whoever does not love remains in death.
Everyone who hates his brother is a murderer,
and you know that no murderer has eternal life remaining in him.
The way we came to know love
was that he laid down his life for us;
so we ought to lay down our lives for our brothers.
If someone who has worldly means
sees a brother in need and refuses him compassion,
how can the love of God remain in him?
Children, let us love not in word or speech
but in deed and truth.

Now this is how we shall know that we belong to the truth
and reassure our hearts before him
in whatever our hearts condemn,
for God is greater than our hearts and knows everything.
Beloved, if our hearts do not condemn us,
we have confidence in God

The word of the Lord.

947C RESPONSORIAL PSALM

1.

Psalm 8:4-5, 6-7, 8-9

℟. (2ab) **O Lord, our God, how wonderful your name in all the earth!**

When I behold your heavens, the work of your fingers,
the moon and stars which you set in place—
What is man that you should be mindful of him,
or the son of man that you should care for him?

℟. **O Lord, our God, how wonderful your name in all the earth!**

You have made him little less than the angels,
and crowned him with glory and honor.
You have given him rule over the works of your hands,
putting all things under his feet.

℟. **O Lord, our God, how wonderful your name in all the earth!**

All sheep and oxen,
yes, and the beasts of the field,
The birds of the air, the fishes of the sea,
and whatever swims the paths of the seas.

℟. **O Lord, our God, how wonderful your name in all the earth!**

2.

Psalm 139:1b-3, 13-14ab, 14c-15

℟. (14) **I praise you, for I am wonderfully made.**

O Lord, you have probed me, you know me:
you know when I sit and when I stand;
you understand my thoughts from afar.
My journeys and my rest you scrutinize;
with all my ways you are familiar.

℟. **I praise you, for I am wonderfully made.**

Truly you have formed my inmost being;
you knit me in my mother's womb.
I give you thanks that I am fearfully, wonderfully made;
wonderful are your works.

℟. **I praise you, for I am wonderfully made.**

My soul also you knew full well;
nor was my frame unknown to you,
When I was made in secret,
when I was fashioned in the depths of the earth.

℟. **I praise you, for I am wonderfully made.**

947D ALLELUIA VERSE AND VERSE BEFORE THE GOSPEL

1.

Psalm 119:88

**In your mercy, give me life, O Lord,
and I will do your commands.**

2.

See John 6:63c, 68c

**Your words, Lord, are Spirit and life;
you have the words of everlasting life.**

3.

See John 17:17b, 17a

**Your word, O Lord, is truth;
consecrate us in the truth.**

947E GOSPEL

First Option

Matthew 18:1-5, 10, 12-14 See that you do not despise one of these little ones.

✠ **A reading from the holy Gospel according to Matthew**

The disciples approached Jesus and said,
"Who is the greatest in the Kingdom of heaven?"
He called a child over, placed it in their midst, and said,
"Amen, I say to you, unless you turn and become like children,
you will not enter the Kingdom of heaven.
Whoever becomes humble like this child
is the greatest in the Kingdom of heaven.
And whoever receives one child such as this in my name
receives me.

"See that you do not despise one of these little ones,
for I say to you that their angels in heaven
always look upon the face of my heavenly Father.
What is your opinion?
If a man has a hundred sheep and one of them goes astray,
will he not leave the ninety-nine in the hills
and go in search of the stray?
And if he finds it, amen, I say to you, he rejoices more over it
than over the ninety-nine that did not stray.
In just the same way, it is not the will of your heavenly Father
that one of these little ones be lost."

The Gospel of the Lord.

Second Option

Mark 9:30-37 The Son of Man is to be handed over . . . Whoever wishes to be first will be the servant of all.

✠ **A reading from the holy Gospel according to Mark**

Jesus and his disciples left from there and began a journey
through Galilee,
but he did not wish anyone to know about it.
He was teaching his disciples and telling them,
"The Son of Man is to be handed over to men
and they will kill him,
and three days after his death the Son of Man will rise."
But they did not understand the saying,
and they were afraid to question him.
They came to Capernaum and, once inside the house,
he began to ask them,
"What were you arguing about on the way?"
But they remained silent.
They had been discussing among themselves on the way
who was the greatest.
Then he sat down, called the Twelve, and said to them,
"If anyone wishes to be first,
he shall be the last of all and the servant of all."
Taking a child, he placed it in their midst,
and putting his arms around it, he said to them,
"Whoever receives one child such as this in my name, receives me;
and whoever receives me,
receives not me but the One who sent me."

The Gospel of the Lord.

Third Option

Luke 1:39-56 The Almighty has done great things for me: he has raised up the lowly.

✠ **A reading from the holy Gospel according to Luke**

Mary set out
and traveled to the hill country in haste
to a town of Judah,
where she entered the house of Zechariah
and greeted Elizabeth.
When Elizabeth heard Mary's greeting,
the infant leaped in her womb,
and Elizabeth, filled with the Holy Spirit,
cried out in a loud voice and said,
"Blessed are you among women,
and blessed is the fruit of your womb.
And how does this happen to me,
that the mother of my Lord should come to me?
For at the moment the sound of your greeting reached my ears,
the infant in my womb leaped for joy.
Blessed are you who believed
that what was spoken to you by the Lord
would be fulfilled."

And Mary said:
"My soul proclaims the greatness of the Lord;
my spirit rejoices in God my Savior
for he has looked with favor upon his lowly servant.
From this day all generations will call me blessed:
the Almighty has done great things for me,
and holy is his Name.
He has mercy on those who fear him
in every generation.

He has shown the strength of his arm,
and has scattered the proud in their conceit.
He has cast down the mighty from their thrones,
and has lifted up the lowly.
He has filled the hungry with good things,
and the rich he has sent away empty.
He has come to the help of his servant Israel
for he has remembered his promise of mercy,
the promise he made to our fathers,
to Abraham and his children for ever."

Mary remained with her about three months
and then returned to her home.

The Gospel of the Lord.

Fourth Option

Luke 17:11-19 None but this foreigner has returned to give thanks to God.

✠ **A reading from the holy Gospel according to Luke**

As Jesus continued his journey to Jerusalem,
he traveled through Samaria and Galilee.
As he was entering a village, ten lepers met him.
They stood at a distance from him and raised their voice, saying,
"Jesus, Master! Have pity on us!"
And when he saw them, he said,
"Go show yourselves to the priests."
As they were going they were cleansed.
And one of them, realizing he had been healed,
returned, glorifying God in a loud voice;
and he fell at the feet of Jesus and thanked him.
He was a Samaritan.
Jesus said in reply,
"Ten were cleansed, were they not?
Where are the other nine?
Has none but this foreigner returned to give thanks to God?"
Then he said to him, "Stand up and go;
your faith has saved you."

The Gospel of the Lord.

Fifth Option

Luke 23:35-43 Lord, remember me when you come into your kingdom.

✠ **A reading from the holy Gospel according to Luke**

The rulers sneered at Jesus and said,
"He saved others, let him save himself
if he is the chosen one, the Christ of God."
Even the soldiers jeered at him.
As they approached to offer him wine they called out,
"If you are King of the Jews, save yourself."
Above him there was an inscription that read,
"This is the King of the Jews."

Now one of the criminals hanging there reviled Jesus, saying,
"Are you not the Christ?
Save yourself and us."
The other, however, rebuking him, said in reply,
"Have you no fear of God,
for you are subject to the same condemnation?
And indeed, we have been condemned justly,
for the sentence we received corresponds to our crimes,
but this man has done nothing criminal."
Then he said,
"Jesus, remember me when you come into your kingdom."
He replied to him,
"Amen, I say to you,
today you will be with me in Paradise."

The Gospel of the Lord.

Sixth Option

John 1:1-5, 9-14, 16-18 He gave power to become children of God to those who believe in his name.

✠ **A reading from the holy Gospel according to John**

In the beginning was the Word,
and the Word was with God,
and the Word was God.
He was in the beginning with God.
All things came to be through him,
and without him nothing came to be.
What came to be through him was life,
and this life was the light of the human race;
the light shines in the darkness,
and the darkness has not overcome it.

The true light, which enlightens everyone, was coming into the world.

He was in the world,
and the world came to be through him,
but the world did not know him.
He came to what was his own,
but his own people did not accept him.

But to those who did accept him
he gave power to become children of God,
to those who believe in his name,
who were born not by natural generation
nor by human choice nor by a man's decision
but of God.

And the Word became flesh
and made his dwelling among us,
and we saw his glory,
the glory as of the Father's only-begotten Son,
full of grace and truth.

From his fullness we have all received,
grace in place of grace,
because while the law was given through Moses,
grace and truth came through Jesus Christ.
No one has ever seen God.
The only-begotten Son, God, who is at the Father's side,
has revealed him.

The Gospel of the Lord.

Seventh Option

John 6:24-35 Whoever comes to me will never hunger, and whoever believes in me will never thirst.

✠ **A reading from the holy Gospel according to John**

When the crowd saw that neither Jesus nor his disciples were there,
they themselves got into boats
and came to Capernaum looking for Jesus.
And when they found him across the sea they said to him,
"Rabbi, when did you get here?"
Jesus answered them and said,
"Amen, amen, I say to you,
you are looking for me not because you saw signs
but because you ate the loaves and were filled.
Do not work for food that perishes
but for the food that endures for eternal life,
which the Son of Man will give you.
For on him the Father, God, has set his seal."
So they said to him,
"What can we do to accomplish the works of God?"
Jesus answered and said to them,
"This is the work of God, that you believe in the one he sent."
So they said to him,
"What sign can you do, that we may see and believe in you?
What can you do?
Our ancestors ate manna in the desert, as it is written:
***He gave them bread from heaven to eat.*"**
So Jesus said to them,
"Amen, amen, I say to you,
it was not Moses who gave the bread from heaven;
my Father gives you the true bread from heaven.

For the bread of God is that which comes down from heaven
and gives life to the world."

So they said to him,
"Sir, give us this bread always."
Jesus said to them,
"I am the bread of life;
whoever comes to me will never hunger,
and whoever believes in me will never thirst."

The Gospel of the Lord.

VOTIVE MASSES

968A THE MERCY OF GOD

FIRST READING

1 Peter 1:3-9 In his great mercy, God has given us new birth to a living hope through the resurrection of Jesus Christ.

A reading from the first Letter of Saint Peter

Blessed be the God and Father of our Lord Jesus Christ,
who in his great mercy gave us a new birth to a living hope
through the resurrection of Jesus Christ from the dead,
to an inheritance that is imperishable, undefiled, and unfading,
kept in heaven for you
who by the power of God are safeguarded through faith,
to a salvation that is ready to be revealed in the final time.
In this you rejoice, although now for a little while
you may have to suffer through various trials,
so that the genuineness of your faith,
more precious than gold that is perishable even though tested by fire,
may prove to be for praise, glory, and honor
at the revelation of Jesus Christ.
Although you have not seen him you love him;
even though you do not see him now yet believe in him,
you rejoice with an indescribable and glorious joy,
as you attain the goal of your faith, the salvation of your souls.

The word of the Lord.

RESPONSORIAL PSALM

Psalm 118:2-4, 13-15, 22-24

℟. (1) **Give thanks to the Lord, for he is good, his love is everlasting.**

Let the house of Israel say,
"His mercy endures forever."
Let the house of Aaron say,
"His mercy endures forever."
Let those who fear the LORD say,
"His mercy endures forever."

℟. **Give thanks to the Lord, for he is good, his love is everlasting.**

I was hard pressed and was falling,
but the LORD helped me.
My strength and my courage is the LORD,
and he has been my savior.
The joyful shout of victory
in the tents of the just.

℟. **Give thanks to the Lord, for he is good, his love is everlasting.**

The stone which the builders rejected
has become the cornerstone.
By the LORD has this been done;
it is wonderful in our eyes.
This is the day the LORD has made;
let us be glad and rejoice in it.

℟. **Give thanks to the Lord, for he is good, his love is everlasting.**

ALLELUIA

See Psalm 145:9

℟. **Alleluia, alleluia.**

The Lord is good to all
and compassionate toward all his works.

℟. **Alleluia, alleluia.**

GOSPEL

First Option

Matthew 20:25b-28 The Son of Man came to give his life as a ransom for many.

✠ **A reading from the holy Gospel according to Matthew**

Jesus summoned his disciples and said,
"You know that the rulers of the Gentiles lord it over them,
and the great ones make their authority over them felt.
But it shall not be so among you.
Rather, whoever wishes to be great among you shall be your servant;
whoever wishes to be first among you shall be your slave.
Just so, the Son of Man did not come to be served
but to serve and to give his life as a ransom for many."

The Gospel of the Lord.

Second Option

John 15:9-14 No one has greater love than this: to lay down one's life for one's friends.

✠ **A reading from the holy Gospel according to John**

Jesus said to his disciples:
"As the Father loves me, so I also love you.
Remain in my love.
If you keep my commandments, you will remain in my love,
just as I have kept my Father's commandments
and remain in his love.

"I have told you this so that my joy might be in you
and your joy might be complete.
This is my commandment: love one another as I love you.
No one has greater love than this,
to lay down one's life for one's friends.
You are my friends if you do what I command you."

The Gospel of the Lord.

The readings for the Votive Mass of the Most Precious Blood of our Lord Jesus Christ, vol. IV, nos. 989–994, or for the Votive Mass of the Most Sacred Heart of Jesus, vol. IV, nos. 995–1000, may also be used.

1002 THE BLESSED VIRGIN MARY

III. OUR LADY, QUEEN OF APOSTLES

The following readings for the Votive Mass of Our Lady, Queen of Apostles may also be used in the Votive Mass for the Blessed Virgin Mary.

FIRST READING

Acts 1:12-14 All these devoted themselves with one accord to prayer with Mary, the mother of Jesus.

A reading from the Acts of the Apostles

After Jesus had been taken up to heaven,
the Apostles returned to Jerusalem
from the mount called Olivet, which is near Jerusalem,
a sabbath day's journey away.

When they entered the city
they went to the upper room where they were staying,
Peter and John and James and Andrew,
Philip and Thomas, Bartholomew and Matthew,
James son of Alphaeus, Simon the Zealot,
and Judas son of James.
All these devoted themselves with one accord to prayer,
together with some women,
and Mary the mother of Jesus, and his brothers.

The word of the Lord.

RESPONSORIAL PSALM

Luke 1:46-47, 48-49, 50-51, 52-52, 54-55

℟. (49) **The Almighty has done great things for me, and holy is his Name.**

or:

℟. **O Blessed Virgin Mary, you carried the Son of the eternal Father.**

"My soul proclaims the greatness of the Lord,
my spirit rejoices in God my savior."

℟. **The Almighty has done great things for me, and holy is his Name.**

or:

℟. **O Blessed Virgin Mary, you carried the Son of the eternal Father.**

"For he has looked with favor on his lowly servant.
From this day all generations will call me blessed:
the Almighty has done great things for me,
and holy is his Name."

℟. **The Almighty has done great things for me, and holy is his Name.**

or:

℟. **O Blessed Virgin Mary, you carried the Son of the eternal Father.**

"He has mercy on those who fear him
in every generation.
He has shown the strength of his arm,
he has scattered the proud in their conceit."

℟. The Almighty has done great things for me, and holy is his Name.

or:

℟. O Blessed Virgin Mary, you carried the Son of the eternal Father.

"He has cast down the mighty from their thrones,
and has lifted up the lowly.
He has filled the hungry with good things,
and the rich he has sent away empty."

℟. The Almighty has done great things for me, and holy is his Name.

or:

℟. O Blessed Virgin Mary, you carried the Son of the eternal Father.

"He has come to the help of his servant Israel
for he has remembered his promise of mercy,
the promise he made to our fathers,
to Abraham and his children for ever."

℟. The Almighty has done great things for me, and holy is his Name.

or:

℟. O Blessed Virgin Mary, you carried the Son of the eternal Father.

ALLELUIA

Luke 11:28

℟. **Alleluia, alleluia.**

Blessed are those who hear the word of God
and observe it.

℟. **Alleluia, alleluia.**

GOSPEL

First Option

Matthew 12:46-50 Stretching out his hand toward his disciples, he said, here are my mother and my brothers.

✠ **A reading from the holy Gospel according to Matthew**

While Jesus was speaking to the crowds,
his mother and his brothers appeared outside,
wishing to speak with him.
Someone told him, "Your mother and your brothers are standing outside,
asking to speak with you."
But he said in reply to the one who told him,
"Who is my mother? Who are my brothers?"
And stretching out his hand toward his disciples, he said,
"Here are my mother and my brothers.
For whoever does the will of my heavenly Father
is my brother, and sister, and mother."

The Gospel of the Lord.

Second Option

John 19:25-27 Behold, your son. Behold, your mother.

✠ **A reading from the holy Gospel according to John**

Standing by the cross of Jesus were his mother
and his mother's sister, Mary the wife of Clopas,
and Mary Magdalene.
When Jesus saw his mother and the disciple there whom he loved,
he said to his mother, "Woman, behold, your son."
Then he said to the disciple,
"Behold, your mother."
And from that hour the disciple took her into his home.

The Gospel of the Lord.

1003A SAINT JOHN THE BAPTIST

The readings for the Solemnity of the Nativity of Saint John the Baptist on June 24, vol. II or III, nos. 586–587, or those for the Memorial of the Passion of Saint John the Baptist, August 29, vol. II or III, no. 634, are used.